# The Barnabas Factor

For Maureen, my wife
and encourager-in-chief

# The
# Barnabas
# Factor

## The power of encouragement

## Derek Wood

Inter-Varsity Press

INTER-VARSITY PRESS
38 De Montfort Street, Leicester LE1 7GP, England

First published 1988
Reprinted 1988, 1989, 1993

British Library Cataloguing in Publication Data
Wood, Derek, 1934-
    The Barnabas factor.
    1. Christian life. Encouragement
    2. Title
    248.4

ISBN 0-85110-480-0

Set in Clearface
Printed and bound in Great Britain by
Cox & Wyman Ltd, Cardiff Road, Reading

Inter-Varsity Press is the book-publishing division of the Universities
and Colleges Christian Fellowship (formerly the Inter-Varsity
Fellowship), a student movement linking Christian Unions in
universities and colleges throughout the United Kingdom and
the Republic of Ireland, and a member movement of the Inter-
national Fellowship of Evangelical Students. For information
about local and national activities write to UCCF, 38 De
Montfort Street, Leicester LE1 7GP.

# Contents

# Foreword

It was Christmas week; the day after our annual carol service. My husband was weary. He still had several Christmas sermons to prepare and was wondering where the resources to prepare and preach them were going to come from when there was a ring at the door bell. He opened the door to find a member of our congregation on the doorstep.

'Before I say anything else,' I heard this young man say, 'I'd like to say how much I appreciated last night's carol service. It all fitted together beautifully. You must have spent a lot of time putting it all together.'

I watched David's reaction. Such affirmation doesn't come his way too often. At first he seemed stunned, then relieved, then delighted. After that, fresh energy seemed to spur him on. Re-energized, he coped well with the remainder of the week.

'And all it took was three sentences of encouragement,' I thought to myself. They were better than a tonic.

But of course it's not only the clergy who need such an injection of new life. We all need it. What's more, we can all give it to one another. That's the main thrust of this light-hearted look at the gift of encouragement, 'the Barnabas factor'. Light-hearted? Yes. But profound too.

Reading the manuscript rekindled in me the desire to become a regular donor of this magic tonic so that people in my circle of friends and acquaintances would be built up by me. I hope that that's happening. What I hadn't bargained for was the personal spin-off the book would have, but I'm finding that as I voice encouragement I'm becoming a happier, more contented person. So I'm grateful for this book of encouragement and believe that many readers will thank God for it too.

Joyce Huggett

# From the author

Ask any group of people who is their favourite Bible character and it won't be long before the name of Barnabas is mentioned. He comes across to us as a warm and attractive personality and, for this reason, is the ideal focus for a book about encouragement.

Much is said about the need for encouragement, but I suspect that not enough is done about it. This is odd because it's such an attractive proposition. It's not like taking unpleasant medicine. I have greatly enjoyed writing this book and my hope is that you will not only enjoy reading it but have delight in putting some of its ideas into practice.

As for the inhabitants of Canwell Park, SW31, they have all become friends of mine as I have recorded their doings over the past months, but I must emphasize that if anyone thinks he sees him or herself in these pages they are mistaken.

My grateful thanks to colleagues, friends and family for their help and encouragement. If this book has any success they will be to a great degree responsible.

Derek Wood

# 1
# The missing ingredient

London's Royal Albert Hall was packed to the roof. Thousands of excited spectators were screaming and yelling encouragement. Under the brilliant lights four female figures were bringing the whole auditorium to fever pitch.

The year was 1978, the occasion, the Wightman Cup, when the top ladies of lawn tennis from the United States and Great Britain confronted each other, with the expectation that Britain would be defeated yet again. But this time, perhaps this time, things might be different. The match was all square and everything depended on the final doubles. On paper the American team was the stronger. Admittedly Pam Shriver was only sixteen, but what does that matter when you are as talented (and as tall) as she is, and have Chris Evert as your partner?

For Great Britain, Virginia Wade and Sue Barker were playing the match of their lives. One set all and the games going with service in the final set. Four all. One supreme effort, two more games, and the Wightman Cup would come to Britain. As their dream came true, and those delirious supporters willed their heroines to win, it seemed that the result was now inevitable. The American team was playing not only two very determined Britishers but a whole Albert Hall full of fans. And how many more (millions?) were urging their team to win as they watched on television?

Only a game of course. Yes, but an example of the power of encouragement. This factor is well known and widely appreciated in the world of sport. Football teams need their supporters to give them vocal backing and many an athlete has been urged over the last hundred metres by a sympathetic crowd.

What is right in sport though is not necessarily right in religion. Will 3,000 worshippers rise to their feet and urge the Archbishop of Canterbury to complete a triumphant sermon? Will the whole congregation cheer lustily as the collection is being taken, willing each other to give sacrificially? Applause is not unknown in church nowadays and, in some circles, sermons are punctuated by fervent 'Aymens' and 'Alleluias' from the congregation, but on the whole religion is not on a par with sport. And rightly so, we may say, they have different purposes. True, but, in practice, the sportsman thrives on encouragement, and the Christian gets very very little. It is not only the means of expression that vary but the quantity and quality of the encouragement. Sometimes it dries up altogether.

# Unworthy sinners or potential saints

The church is hushed and the preacher is driven by an unseen power to greater and greater flights of oratory. The Christian congregation is on the rack. The preacher has been a pioneer missionary of the old school. Turning his back on a comfortable home and a promising career he had immersed himself in a remote mountain area of Umbola, lived a life of almost incredible hardship and bravely faced the fact that no convert has yet been made there.

Now, becoming fragile with advancing age, he appeals to the many young people before him to reflect on the sinfulness of the inhabitants of the remote area of Umbola and also upon their own moral worthlessness. He holds out to them the desperate need for new waves of young people to sacrifice themselves in areas like those and also speaks of their total unworthiness. Guilt is written clearly on every face as the preacher concludes his address. A thousand excuses course through a hundred minds as they pause in silence to consider God's call. And a hundred guilty souls creep out to continue their promising careers from comfortable homes, but carrying with them the dubious luxury of a guilty conscience.

Exaggeration? Yes of course, but is there not a grain or two of truth among the chaff? Is the preacher correct to draw attention to the sinfulness of that remote people? Of course he is. And are his hearers really unworthy? Yes, they really are. But the point is, has he approached them in the best way? Has he *encouraged* them to understand what a loving God wants of them?

What does the preacher see as he looks round upon that sea of faces? A room filled with unworthy sinners. He sees himself as an unworthy sinner. And he's right on both counts. But does he also see a room full of potential saints? Does he view himself as a worm in the service of God or as the apple of God's eye? Because they *are* potential, if not actual, saints and he *is* the apple of God's eye and there is joy in the challenge and true happiness in the sacrifice.

The fact is that a strong and unrelieved emphasis on the unworthiness of the Christian and the demand for more and more effort and self-sacrifice leave us crushed and weak. We come to see others as either contemptible or so much more holy than ourselves that we despair of attaining to their standard. We see God as the man in the parable saw him—a 'hard man', demanding the last ounce out of us and so, like that

13

servant who was given only one talent, we are afraid of the Lord and instead of joyfully using our gift we hide it in terror of his judgment (Luke 19:11-27).

We see a half-full glass as half-empty.

We are discouraged. We lack the grace of being encouraged and we fear to encourage each other.

## Whose side are you on?

Look back for a moment to the tennis match and compare it with the caricature of the preacher. They are both extreme cases, but the comparison may be instructive. In the first case two people were being encouraged by thousands. In the second case one man was addressing hundreds. In the tennis match, the girls were being urged to continue to do what they were doing and to do it even better. In the church, the congregation was being asked to begin to do something it didn't wish to do.

But the most significant difference is this: the tennis players and the crowd were united, flowing together in a tide of purpose. But the preacher and his audience appeared to be on opposite sides. He was attacking and they were mentally defending themselves. In a situation where you might expect Christians to be exhibiting their loving unity it would be possible to ask, 'Whose side are you on, ours or his?'

If I didn't believe in the existence of Satan I should have to invent him at this point, to explain how it is that Christians, of all people, can be so suspicious of each other, so negative in their ideas about God, so fearful, so hesitant and so critical of everyone who sees things differently from the way they do. And so *discouraging*.

## 'Encourage one another'

When did someone last encourage you—make you feel genuinely appreciated and needed? I am not talking about formal thanks after a talk ('that was very interesting. I'm sure we've been given a lot to think about', which, being interpreted, means, 'I didn't understand it and it was too long'). I am not

14

talking about flattery or exaggeration, but simple affirmation that made you feel needed and wanted. Too frequently our fellow Christians make us feel small, unworthy, incompetent or, at best, in need of care and attention. The Bible cannot be the source of this devaluation process. John's gospel narrative, for instance, was written so that his readers should 'believe that Jesus is the Christ, the Son of God, and that by believing you may have life in his name' (John 20:31). Nothing negative there.

The life of Jesus is full of examples of how he encouraged, forgave, strengthened and healed the people he met.

The New Testament letters echo to the cry of encouragement. What do you think of Paul? A tight-lipped little man who went about correcting people's wrong beliefs? How about this:

> *I long to see you so that I may impart to you some spiritual gift to make you strong—that is, that you and I may be mutually encouraged by each other's faith.*
>
> (Romans 1:11-12).

Then look at the list of people to whom he sends his love at the end of Romans, in chapter 16.

In his final greetings to the Ephesians Paul writes:

> *I am sending him (Tychicus) to you for this very purpose, that you may know how we are, and that he may encourage you.*
>
> (Ephesians 6:22).

The writer to the Hebrews couldn't wait until the next Sunday's service for a bit of encouragement. He wrote, 'Encourage one another daily' (Hebrews 3:13) and 'let us consider how we may spur one another on towards love and good deeds. Let us not give up meeting together...but let us encourage one another...' (Hebrews 10:24-25).

The Bible is not alone in advocating encouragement. The

German poet Goethe wrote, 'Correction does much, but encouragement does more...Encouragement after censure is as the sun after a shower'. Writer George Adams put it even more simply, 'Encouragement is oxygen to the soul'.

Encouragement is certainly good and beneficial. And if you are fortunate enough to feel totally affirmed, utterly needed and regularly encouraged, that's fine. But is it possible that you are sometimes discouraged, lacking in self-confidence, unsure of God's love or anybody else's? Welcome to the human race! But don't leave it there. Let's look a little further because this question of encouraging and being encouraged is something that we *can* do something about. Let's consider more specifically who needs encouragement.

> Is encouragement the missing ingredient in your fellowship/group/place of work/family?
> What might you do about it?

# 2
# Who needs encouraging?

**A**t first glance, some people seem to be in special need of encouragement. A brief visit to any school for handicapped children for instance, will give you one emphatic example.

Children who have grown up with their handicaps are wonderfully able to cope with them, but if you are confined to a wheelchair and have to be carried from car to chair in the morning and back from chair to car in the evening; if you can't see clearly and can't communicate except through a board attached to a tray in front of your chair; if you can't write except by means of a word processor and that if your school can afford enough to go round; if you are conscious that you have a progressive disease that means you cannot realistically expect to live beyond the age of twenty, then you need encouragement. Not to be patronized but encouraged.

It may be the encouragement of being treated as any other young person of the same age would be treated, or just a simple 'well done' or a shake of the hand. It is heartwarming to read the thanks in the eyes of a child who can neither speak nor write, but has been appreciated for being himself and doing something positive.

Their teachers need encouragement too. Faced with all the stresses involved with coaxing the unwilling to learn, grappling with regulations for new examinations, harried by the call to industrial action and all manner of distractions, teachers need encouragement. And most of the non-handicapped children are more of a threat than the handicapped.

## Who encourages the boss?

It's common enough to be told how frustrating it is to be unemployed, but stop for a moment and think again about the desperate feeling of rejection experienced by someone whom nobody seems to want—whose role in life is... nothing. If anyone needs encouraging, it must be the unemployed.

Perhaps so, but I can hear plenty of people who have jobs saying at this point, 'Fine, yes I've got a job and I suppose I'm providing a service, or doing something useful but nobody ever *tells* me so. I'm not asking for praise, certainly not public reward, but if only someone would say occasionally, "Well done" or "It's good to have you here with us". It would make all the difference.'

Of course that happens in some well-regulated situations. The employees are made to feel wanted and needed and the atmosphere is good. People like working there. The section heads affirm their colleagues— it's company policy, and the boss tells the section heads what a good job they're doing; not too often, but just enough. But who encourages the boss? He is expected to be the source of encouragement, but that particular buck, like so many others, stops on his desk. If his employees admire him they can't easily say so. It might appear that they are angling for promotion.

So he or she is expected to give and in return rest in the satisfaction of being the boss. With the responsibility that goes with the job, is that satisfaction enough? In any case, too often the boss/employee situation is another 'us and them' contest, where the underdog is glad to see the top dog knocked off the roof of his kennel occasionally.

So let's get out of the unpleasant atmosphere of competition in the secular business world and enjoy a taste of a warm fellowship. What is it like in a church where the members are committed to helping each other? No competition here, no jockeying for position, no trying to push ourselves forward at the expense of others.

# One Sunday morning

The time is 11.15. The family service has just finished and the church is alive with small groups of people drinking coffee and relaxing together before going home for Sunday lunch. It could be any late-twentieth-century congregation engaged in mutual encouragement. It *could* be. But is it? Focus in on some of the groups and turn up the volume so that we can hear what they're saying.

Here are three people near the bookstall. The vicar, the Revd Timothy Monteith, is in earnest conversation over coffee with church treasurer Gordon Barber. Six-year-old Shelley Barber is standing next to them, or rather hopping from one foot to the other, waving a piece of paper from side to side above her head, obviously trying to attract Daddy's attention.

Gordon, tall, prematurely bald and dressed in a green jacket, is explaining to Timothy something that has been concerning him for some time, the fact that the church's missionary giving has not kept pace with inflation, while running expenses on the home front have exceeded budget by 7% so far this year. This is all the more disturbing, as he emphasizes with great earnestness, because St Peter's have just had a missionary gift day and announced a record offering. Shouldn't we be doing the same?

Timothy has two problems. The first is that every mention of St Peter's sends a cold shiver down his back. Must his church members keep comparing his performance with that of the vicar of St Peter's? St Peter's is the 'successful church' (whatever that may mean). 'Of course at *St Peter's* they have 300 to morning service' and 'their vicar is *very* good with the youth, you know.' It isn't meant that way, but every mention of St Peter's feels like a criticism of his own ministry.

In addition, Timothy, looking older than his thirty-seven years, has just preached a sermon which has drained him emotionally. He has shared more of himself than ever before and has invited a response from the congregation. He glances round. Nobody is waiting to see him. Nobody seems to want to follow up his plea for more warm-hearted openness. Meanwhile here is Gordon, going on and on about their failure to live up to St Peter's and its missionary-minded reputation.

Gordon, of course, is totally unconscious of the pain he is causing, his mind full of balance sheets and thank you letters from missionary societies. Unconscious too of the still-waving arm of daughter Shelley, three feet below the level of his attention.

Shelley has been fired with enthusiasm in her class this morning and has covered the whole of her sheet of paper with coloured cut-outs of Mummies, Daddies, potted plants, a cat and the sun. Her teacher has asked them to make a picture to show how much they love their family and she has been bursting to give her offering of love to her Daddy ever since she finished it twenty minutes before. She goes on waving her picture. Daddy goes on discussing missionary giving. Timothy goes on suffering.

# Women's meeting

In a corner of the church, next to the radiator, there appears to be a women's meeting in progress: Gina Holwell, dark-haired, a widow, forty-five and full of vigour, wiry and tough, an indefatigable church worker; Vivien James, twenty-eight, married, an infant teacher, extremely diffident and unable to see any good in herself, full of admiration for everyone else; Jane Goodrich, unmarried, sixty-three, who has spent most of her life nursing her invalid mother, who is now entering her ninety-fifth year; and Margaret Barber, wife of Gordon. Her problem is that she cannot see the love of God at work in the world. Everywhere she sees suffering and pain. Her mind is filled with doubt; aren't the missionaries really wasting their lives?

As is sometimes the manner of groups of four, the members have separated into pairs, but are talking to each other simultaneously, diagonally across the line of each other's conversations.

Jane is trying to persuade Vivien that she has lots to be proud of and shouldn't be so self-effacing. Hasn't she got a loving husband and a good job? Oughtn't she to pull herself together and walk six inches taller and show everyone that she counts? Vivien has heard all this before, at least once a week, on Sunday mornings, and says humbly, 'Yes, I suppose you're right, thank you', while she thinks, 'If you go on about walking six inches taller any more I shall *scream!*'

Jane is talking on automatic, repeating what she has said many times before. Her mind is in that bedroom, half a mile away, occupied by her mother and herself. If only someone would come in once a week—if only someone would ask her how she's getting on even—if only she didn't have to support Vivien all the time—if only Vivien would support *her* for a change.

Gina is 'helping' Margaret to resolve her doubts, very aggressively and very loudly, telling her to trust the Lord, trust the Bible, commit herself fully and her problems will roll away. Margaret is trying desperately to be grateful for Gina's concern but finding no comfort at all in this tirade of challenge. It only makes matters worse. 'I *have* believed, I *have* trusted, I *am* committed...I think.'

Deep inside Gina, very deep inside, so deep that she can't hear it, a small voice is weeping. 'Andrew, Andrew. If only you were still here.'

21

On a seat in the middle of the church sits old Mrs Staindrop, also with a cup of coffee. She is glad that someone has noticed her enough to give her a cup (she can't move until her husband calls with the car at 11.30), but she wonders why nobody has time to talk to her.

Young Gavin Morrison is staring blankly at the bookstall. He is pleased with himself because he thought of giving Mrs Staindrop a cup of coffee, and she was so delighted. He thought she looked a bit disappointed when he said he was sorry he was so busy and couldn't stop to chat. And now he's staring at the bookstall wondering what to do.

Bob Renshaw knows what he wants to do—get home. But he has been waylaid at the door by one of the elders who feels responsible for the church's image, and for Bob. For does Bob not spend Tuesday evening in the pub? And is that the *best* place for a Christian to be? Bob happens to believe that it is, not least because he meets an old friend there who won't dream of coming to church, but who loves conversation, and they often gather a group to talk about matters of moment in a quiet corner. Bob listens to the embarrassed elder, excuses himself and walks home. He is not encouraged.

11.30, and the church is emptying. Warm greetings, friendly handshakes, 'See you Tuesday'. People with the best of intentions, each contributing to the destruction of the others. Christian people, but very largely self-centred people, unable or unwilling to learn what other people's needs really are.

Who, then, needs encouragement? The handicapped, the teachers, the unemployed, the employed, the employers, the clergy, the treasurers, the children, the elderly, the bereaved, those with a poor self-image, those who have suffered greatly, the doubters, the shy...

Not only all those, but many many more, in other words everybody, without any exception. We all need encouragement and we all need to offer it to others. Yet so many of us seem unable to begin to do it. And when we do we make a mess of it. What a wretched situation! Is there nothing that we can do? Is there no pattern for us to follow, no example of how it should be done?

At this point, enter right and move to centre stage a Levite farmer named Joseph the Cypriot. *Who*? Never heard of him? Perhaps you have. His other name is Barnabas, which means 'Son of encouragement'. He is almost a personification of encouragement. And it's so much easier (and more encouraging!) to meet a person than to read a set of abstract principles.

---

Are you sure that you're not hurting someone by the way you try to help them?
How could you find out?

---

# 3

# Enter Joseph the Cypriot

So, meet Barnabas, Joseph the Cypriot, a Levite. He steps into the pages of history in Acts 4:36-37. He is a Jew. I imagine him as a large, smiling man with a twinkle in his eye, a bushy black beard, and a vice-like handshake, but the records are silent about his appearance.

He is a Levite, not a priest. Levites inherited no land in Israel but represented the people in worship and assisted the priests. The details are in Exodus 2 and 6, Numbers 18 and Deuteronomy 12, but that is beside our purpose here. He is obviously a landowner, so to avoid breaking the law he must have held his property in his native Cyprus.

Names meant a lot to the Jew and I can see why. They were

intended to express the character of the bearer of the name.

Joseph was a good enough name to start with. It seems to have meant 'may he (God) add (sons)'. Genesis 30:24 explains why Rachel gave her son that name. But it wasn't good enough for the young church at Jerusalem. This Joseph obviously became a Christian very early. Perhaps he was one of the people present at Pentecost. Anyway he soon became well known to the apostles and they gave him his new name, Barnabas, 'son of encouragement' or 'son of exhortation'. The word for encouragement here is *paraklēsis*. It doesn't just mean patting people on the head and telling them they're doing fine and the weather forecast is good for the day after tomorrow. The same word is used, as a verb, in 2 Corinthians 8:4 and is translated 'urgently pleaded'. There's more than a touch of vigour and drive in this word.

To encourage someone is to give them good reasons for feeling better or doing greater things, and it may involve some persuasion too. It is no accident that the word 'exhort' is used in the older versions as well as 'console' to express the double meaning of *propelling someone in the right direction*.

# Dispositionally negative?

So why did the apostles call Joseph 'Barnabas'? Because he was a born encourager? Perhaps so. Or was it because they wanted him to *improve* as an encourager, so they gave him the name and thus encouraged him to live up to his new reputation? This idea is not as far-fetched as it may sound. Roger Mitchell has this interesting theory:

> Many people say that they have the wrong disposition to be encouragers. But it is not a question of natural disposition, but of spiritual gift. I think it quite likely that Barnabas was dispositionally a negative person to start with and that the apostles called him 'Son of encouragement' to get him out of it. This is not just an argument from silence. The last thing that Simon, son of Jonas

25

*was, was a rock! But Jesus surnamed him Peter,*
*a rock. Similarly James and John, the sons of*
*Zebedee, were dispositionally wimpish enough to*
*get their mum to ask Jesus for the good places*
*in the coming kingdom. But he called them 'Sons*
*of thunder'. Spiritual gifts flow out of being filled*
*with the Holy Spirit and obeying his lead. We need*
*to break through our natural dispositions and*
*inclinations into his way of doing things.*

('Encouragement': Roger Mitchell, *Cubit*,
Spring 1987)

Whether Barnabas got his name because he was already an
encourager we shall never know, but Roger Mitchell has a
point. Give a dog a bad name and hang him. But give a dog
a good name and you will encourage him to be a better dog.
People really do respond to our expectations of them (provided
we are not so demanding as to crush them). If you tell someone
often enough that he is an encourager you will help him on
the way to being one, or being a better one. Gifts of the Spirit
should be reinforced by practice and by other people's
expectations.

## Learning to give

Our first impression of Barnabas is not complete without a
mention of his generosity. He 'sold a field he owned and
brought the money and put it at the apostles' feet' (Acts 4:37).
This was obviously the done thing at the time. Verses 32-35
explain the primitive form of communism which the young
church practised. Christians sold their belongings and shared
the proceeds, so nobody suffered poverty. The fact that other
people were doing it helped, no doubt, but doesn't mean that
it was easy. It was a very generous act, the act of a generous
man—one who was open-hearted, willing to act deliberately
and decisively.

Ananias and Sapphira, we discover by reading on a few
verses, were a husband and wife team with a rather different

approach. They compromised by selling property and bringing only some of the proceeds, keeping the rest for themselves. Fair enough! you cry. Yes but worse than that, they covered up their consciences and lied about the whole thing. And they paid a rather spectacular price for their ill-conceived foray into the spiritual land-market.

Barnabas wasn't perfect, as we shall see. He was as human as the rest of us, but his generosity was transparent. To be an encourager one needs to be open-hearted and open-handed. Encouragement cannot be projected out of a tight-fisted meanness. It doesn't ring true that way. Before we can give encouragement we may have to learn to give other things, and supremely, to give ourselves.

## 'What's gen'rous?'

Gordon Barber was singing to himself as he left home for the train on Monday morning. It was a normal looking Monday morning—dull, wet and gloomy—and the inhabitants of Canwell Park, London SW31 were also dull, wet and gloomy. But Gordon had something rather special in his briefcase. As he reflected on it he couldn't understand why he should feel so very happy about it. It was quite ordinary really, but it was something enormously encouraging. It was a piece of paper with coloured cut-outs of Mummies, Daddies, potted plants, a cat and the sun and the words, DADY I LOV YOU LOV SHELLEY X scrawled across the sky. Gordon was going to pin it to the chipboard on his office wall. And if his colleagues noticed it, so much the better.

So Shelley had given Gordon her picture. Well no, actually she hadn't. The story is much more complicated. We have to return to Sunday lunch-time...

The atmosphere at the Barber residence was rather brittle. 'Why is it,' thought Margaret, 'that after being at church, of all places, we feel worse than when we left the house? We shall feel fine after lunch, but that's the effect of good food. Where is the "joy of the Lord" that these people keep on about? And why oh why do I have to keep bumping into Gina Holwell?'

Thus mused Margaret over the gravy while Gordon drained the fat from the meat dish and set about dismembering the chicken. He chopped off a leg with evident relish.

'You know,' he said, 'I don't believe Timothy listens to a word you say to him. I don't think he *wants* to listen. I was talking to him after the service about the missionary giving and trying to sell him the St Peter's gift day idea and he didn't bat an eyelid. In fact he kept looking round as if he was trying to escape or something. I can't understand what goes on in his mind. Whenever you talk to him he seems to be somewhere else. It's as if he was where you are a few minutes ago and he's left just before you get there.'

'Stuffing,' said Margaret.

'What?'

'Stuffing. It's still inside the chicken. Do concentrate, dear.'

'Sorry. I was getting at Timothy. Right, let's start. SHELLEY! Come on darling, up to the table. Now let's say thank you to Jesus. "Thank you, Lord Jesus, for all good things, especially for our dinner, and please make us generous. Amen." '

'That's a new one,' said Margaret. 'Why the bit about being generous?'

'I don't know, it seemed to come from somewhere. I think it's because I'm so steamed up about this missionary effort. Why are people so tight-fisted? We've all got more than we need and we can't seem to raise a few hundred pounds. Darling, this chicken is delicious, what did you cook it in?'

'Daddy!'

'Yes, pet.'

'What's gen'rous?'

'Generous. It means giving things away. It means not being selfish with what you have.'

'Does Jesus want us to give things away?'

'Yes dear, he does. Not just throw them away, but he loves it when we take something a bit special and give it to someone who hasn't got one themselves. Like giving a toy to someone who's in hospital at Christmas. Now eat up your chicken. We've got chocolate mousse next...'

Shelley became very thoughtful and surprisingly quiet. After lunch her friend Sarah from next door asked her to come and play so Gordon and Margaret gratefully accepted the offer of two hours' peace and quiet. Shelley had some difficulty putting on her jacket. There seemed to be something inside the sleeve, but she finally left and silence descended on the house.

# Make another

Two hours later Gordon rang the bell of number 36. 'Come in Gordon, Shelley's ready to come home any minute now. How's Margaret? I hope her cold's better...'

But Gordon was looking at the wall. Grandpa Dale, Sarah's grandfather, lived with the family and above his chair by the fire was a picture composed of coloured cut-outs of Daddies and Mummies and potted plants and a cat and the sun. And it had written on the sky, 'DADY I LOV YOU LOV SHELLEY X'.

Shelley saw him looking at it. 'That's nice,' said Gordon, as cheerfully as he could. 'Have you done that this afternoon?'

'No Daddy, I did it in church this morning. It was for you really, but you didn't want it. And then you said that Jesus wants us to be gen'rous so I gave it to Grandpa Dale because he hasn't got a daughter and you have.'

Gordon was telling Margaret about this episode over tea. Margaret was shocked. 'Shelley! Why did you give Daddy's present away? He may think you don't love him any more.'

Shelley's eyes filled with tears.

'But you said that we should be gen'rous,' she said, 'and I tried to give Daddy his picture this morning but he was busy talking so he didn't take it. So I thought he wouldn't mind.'

Gordon hugged Shelley. 'That's very kind of you, to think of Grandpa Dale like that,' he said. 'I'm sorry I was too busy to talk to you after church. What shall we do now before bed?'

'We'll make another picture of Mummies and Daddies, even nicer than the first one, and it can be for you, Daddy, because I love you.'

Not very profound? In some ways no. In some ways as profound as a simple family happening can be.

Gordon Barber was singing to himself as he left home for the train on Monday morning...

---

Are you ready to *receive* encouragement when it is offered?
Does it embarrass you when you are thanked or affirmed,
praised or encouraged?
Why?

---

# 4
# Building bridges

**B**y the time he was halfway home that evening Gordon had stopped singing. For one thing the trains were packed and he had let two go so that he could get a seat on the third and he was now late. But he needed the seat. He wanted to think.

Why *was* it that he had felt, and still felt, so delighted about little Shelley and the card she had given him? It really had made his day, and yet it was something so simple and so ordinary. Didn't daughters usually love their fathers and didn't they often express their love? Why was he so moved? What was going on?

It occurred to him that one reason for the warm glow in which he had been living all day was that the encouragement had a reason behind it. It was not just the 'cheer up, it may never happen' variety, but 'be strong because I love you'. He *meant* something to someone. The love even of a six-year-old was able to do that.

And was there something significant in this encouragement coming just at a time when Gordon had felt at odds with his minister? Margaret had seemed upset too. She always was. She had so many doubts when everything seemed as clear as day to him. It had been strange that he had used that phrase 'please make us generous' too. All these things taken together began to make Gordon think that Someone was trying to say something to him. Exactly what? He could but ask. 'Father, if you are trying to say something to me, make me listen.'

Before he could even say 'Amen' to his own prayer, the train pulled in, the passengers piled out and he was back in Canwell Park, not quite as damp as it had been in the morning when he'd left it, but otherwise very much the same as ever. As he crossed the road he caught sight of Cyril Kent, the church elder, dark coat, tightly rolled unbrella, tightly shut lips. 'Dear old Cyril. He's not part of the twentieth century yet. And yet he won't change now. He *is* old. He must be getting on for 80. But he is dear too. To somebody. To Edith. And to God. But not to poor Bob. Bob had another earful on Sunday after the service. I saw them at it. Good old Bob. Well, he's not so old. But he is good. Funny. Cyril is 'dear'. Bob is 'good'. But they don't get on together at all. Chalk and cheese they are. They need someone to get them together. That's what they need. Someone... "If you are trying to say something to me, make me listen..." *Me*? I couldn't, Lord, no, not me.'

Gordon collided with his own front gate and fitted his key thoughtfully into the lock.

# Bound in black

Margaret got up to turn down the volume on the TV. It was a musical interlude in the middle of *Wogan*. Gordon said,

'Mag., did you see old Cyril having a go at Bob on Sunday morning?'

'Oh, not *again!*' said Margaret. She liked Bob. He had his convictions and stuck to them. Cyril did too, but Cyril's convictions were too restrictive for her.

'I think someone ought to do something for them both. A church is supposed to be a place of reconciliation and peace.'

'You won't get Cyril to be reconciled to anything or anybody, unless it's bound in black and says "thou shalt not" all over it.'

'But Margaret, he's human, underneath all that. Have you ever spoken to him and got to know him? He's probably quite a nice old stick.'

'Old stick is right,' said Margaret firmly, 'but Cyril Kent is not the kind of person you get to *know*. You are acquainted with him or you have been introduced to him, but nobody could know him.'

'What about Edith?'

'Poor soul! Edith! It must be like living with an iceberg. He wears cuff-links and collar studs. He's in the last century.'

'I know you don't like him. I suppose it's only making things worse to talk about him. I wonder...I wonder whether he would respond to a bit of encouragement.'

'*Encouragement?* What is there to encourage? There's nothing to get hold of. No. I don't think he'll ever change now. He's too far gone. I shouldn't say it and I know God can do anything, but I can't see how even God can change old Cyril. Yes, I know it shocks you and I'm sorry, but that's what I think. Now your favourite daughter wants her bedtime story, and, as you are the sunshine of her little life at the moment I suggest you go and tell it to her. She says I don't do them properly any more and my prayers aren't good enough.'

Margaret turned up the television unnecessarily loud and sat down harder than she need have done.

Story and prayers finished, Gordon said goodnight to Shelley. 'Shelley, you know old Mr Kent don't you?'

'Yes.'

'I think he's sad.'

'Yes.'

'What do you think would cheer him up?'

Shelley's brown eyes were big with concentration on this

33

difficult problem. Then she said,

'Tell him you love him.'

'Good grief!' said Gordon, slapping his forehead with his hand and leaping up. 'I couldn't do that!'

But the discussion was over. Gordon's involuntary gesture sent Shelley into peals of laughter. 'Say good grief again, Daddy,' she said, breathless with mirth. 'Say it again!'

'Shelley!' It was Margaret's irate voice. 'Why aren't you asleep? And why is Daddy getting you all excited?'

But the irritability had gone by the time she had climbed the stairs, and the family goodnight was a picture of contentment.

Except that Shelley said 'good grief' instead of 'good night'. And chuckled herself to sleep.

# Dry old stick

Cyril Kent came to the door wearing a comfortable-looking olive green cardigan. His soft shirt was open at the neck.

'Good evening, Gordon. Why, this is a surprise! Do come in. Excuse my appearance. I'd retired for the night...oh no, no, I don't mean I was going to bed, I mean I had shut the door on the world, you know. Come and share some cocoa. Edith! *Edith*! We have a visitor. This *is* a surprise.'

Gordon had made three attempts to walk up to the Kents' door and twice in the darkness he had turned back because he couldn't face it. Now, after succeeding at the third attempt (he had knocked very softly and hoped nobody would hear), he was being escorted to a warm fireside by a friendly old gentleman who seemed genuinely glad to see him. And here was Edith. Surely not knitting before the fire? Yes, knitting. *And* there was a cat. Gordon looked for a bronze kettle steaming on the hearth, but it seemed that the kettle was electric and in the kitchen.

'People so rarely call, you know,' Cyril was saying, 'it's a great pleasure to see someone, even if he is the church treasurer! It is about money, I suppose. Do have this seat. The other one's collapsible. Edith's sister sat through it last September...'

'July.'

It was the first time Edith had spoken, but her hearing was not as bad as her husband had imagined.

'It was July,' she said, 'when Gladys and Albert came by on their way to Broadstairs.'

'Last July,' said Cyril. 'Well, why not? It won't mend the chair anyway. But what can I do for you, Gordon?'

'Let me come straight to the point then,' said Gordon. 'It's Bob I've come about. Is there any way I can help you to see each other's point of view? I may be wrong, but it looks to me as if you are on different wavelengths. And it can't be very pleasant for either of you.'

Cyril looked surprised.

'I hope you haven't come to give me a lecture on being too much of a Puritan!'

Suddenly Cyril looked furled up like his umbrella.

'Are you trying to convert me to Bob's point of view?'

'No, no,' said Gordon, hastily. 'It's not my job to tell you what to do. You are the elder. It's your job to tell us what we should do...'

'But most of you don't take any notice of a dry old stick like me.'

Where had Gordon heard that before?

'No. I've come to ask you to tell me, if you will, why you are so against Bob going to the pub and why you can't get on with him.'

Edith had returned with cocoa and was looking earnestly at her husband's face.

'Tell him, Cyril,' she said.

Cyril looked hard at the fire for some moments and then spoke so quietly that Gordon had to strain to hear.

'Edith and I had a son, Graham. You never met him of course. We brought him up as a good Christian but we tried to let him find his own way. I couldn't bear the idea of dominating him as my father did me. Temperance. Band of Hope. Signing the pledge. It made a rebel out of me. You may find that strange. But I came back and I wanted my son to enjoy life. We drank a bit at home, you know, sherry before

35

supper and something a bit stronger at Christmas. Graham went to the pub and enjoyed his beer.

'When he left home, Graham went to university and got involved with drink. It just took hold of him. He became an alcoholic. His life fell to pieces. All that promise and nothing left. He died about ten years ago. He was forty-three. Fortunately he never married...'

There was a very long pause. Cyril lifted his eyes to Gordon's.

'Are you surprised that we try to get Bob out of the public house? We are very fond of Bob, you know. We see him...well, he reminds us of Graham.'

Gordon could hardly speak. At length he said, 'Have you ever told Bob all this?'

'No, he wouldn't listen. I can't get near him. But I try. I do try.'

'I've admired you from a distance for a long time,' said Gordon, 'but this evening you've let me come closer. I'm very grateful to you. I feel as if we've met for the first time.'

'I think it's done me good to get it out. We've never talked about it. But you can tell Bob if you like. It might help.'

## Esteem them very highly in love

Some days later Cyril and Edith were sitting by the same fireside with a Bible, open to 1 Thessalonians, on the table between them.

'It all makes sense,' Cyril was saying, 'since Gordon told us why Bob goes to the pub. I wish Bob had told us himself.'

'But you admitted that you hadn't told him why you were so shocked about his going. You were both being rather pigheaded, you know.'

'Yes, I suppose you're right. And it needed Gordon to come between us and build the bridge. This passage from 1 Thessalonians says it all—I never cease to be amazed at how relevant the Bible can be:

' "And we beseech you, brethren, to know them which labour among you and are over you in the Lord, and admonish you; and to esteem them very highly in love for their work's sake.

And be at peace among yourselves."

'What was it he said? "I've admired you from a distance for a long time." "Esteem them very highly in love." That's how it works, you know, Edith. He wouldn't have come to see us if he didn't think something of us. Does that sound sentimental? It does, but it's true!'

The following Sunday, after church, Cyril and Bob are deep in conversation, like a long-lost father and son reunited after years of separation.

And Shelley Barber is waiting for her parents to take her home. She is jumping from one black paving stone to the next black one, and occasionally slapping her head with her hand and muttering, 'Good grief!'.

---

Are you so convinced that you should never poke your nose into other people's business that you will never be a bridge-builder?
Who gave you the right to be so detached?

---

# 5
# Triangular encouragement

**R**econciling two people who have been at odds with each other is one of the ways in which God makes his presence felt. Jesus died to reconcile us to God and the Holy Spirit works in us to bring people back together too. He also works to bring together people who have never met, who wouldn't seem likely ever to want to meet, and gets them working and worshipping alongside each other, *and enjoying it*.

Bridge-building of this kind is triangular-shaped encouragement. It is the Barnabas factor at work between people as well as inside them. And encouragement is one of the best means of getting people together.

Cyril Kent proved to be very easy to help. Sometimes it works like that. All you need to do is to be bold enough to take the initial step, to cut through the other person's reserve with a word or two of encouragement or a demonstration of obvious concern, and the defences crumble and a bridge is built in their place.

There were a few awkward moments. Cyril supposed that Gordon had come about money, and then, when Gordon had taken the plunge, he reacted rather sharply to the younger man's implied criticism. It had been almost worse when he had opened the gates of his private, family history and poured it out to Gordon. Embarrassing really. Yet how very positive and healing it had all turned out to be. Gordon decided that it had been no coincidence that when he had prayed to be guided to someone who needed help, the first person he had seen was Cyril. And what about Shelley's 'tell him that you love him'? In effect he had done more or less that. In his own words. It was all very satisfying.

# Right ideas for the wrong reasons

Some people would describe Gordon as lucky. Sometimes the first real attempt you make to help someone has a much less happy ending (or beginning as it was for Cyril and Bob). Cyril needed only one gentle push and he was off. Others will not budge even if you collide with them head on. In fact, of course, the harder you collide with them, the firmer they become. Why is this? Is it that some people, like Cyril, are soft underneath their crusty exterior and are easily persuaded, while others hold more firmly to their principles?

Not necessarily. Cyril was a man of firm principles and he didn't abandon any of them. His objection to Bob's habits had a perfectly reasonable and practical foundation, once it was uncovered. What seemed like prejudice was really deep concern for Bob. It was an uninformed and defensive concern, which expressed itself too abruptly, so Bob was put off. Cyril's principles were not being threatened; but his feelings were.

'Threatened.' That's a clue. The people who are difficult to reason with usually react sharply to criticism or challenge because they feel threatened. They feel they have something that will be lost if they give in. They become edgy and defensive and sometimes irritable and argumentative. They will argue shrilly that they are holding to matters of principle and will not budge an inch.

You often meet someone who has emotional and insecure reasons for their opinions (they are based on feelings), defending them *as if* they are logical, rational and based on Scripture. They don't realize what is happening. They are very insecure. So any argument brought against their opinions they take as a personal affront. They become more and more irrational in their attempts to be reasonable. And it cannot be done. They are trying to justify emotional opinions by rational arguments. You might as well play tennis with a frying pan. That is bad enough, but when challenged, it is sad in the extreme to pretend that you really are holding a tennis racket.

## Unnecessarily aggressive

If someone has dug himself into that kind of hole, it is very difficult indeed to get him out of it. He doesn't want to come out, for a start, and will easily take fright and dig himself in deeper if threatened with a helping hand. How can we help such people to be more open—to relate to those of differing viewpoints? How can we build the bridges?

You can usually tell when someone is feeling threatened because he becomes stiff and abrupt in manner, clenches his fists or twists the corner of a handkerchief, perhaps talks too fast or too loudly and generally appears unnecessarily aggressive.

There is little point in trying to persuade your friend rationally that he is wrong, because, as we have seen, his position is not based on reason anyway. Even if you do win the argument by sheer force of logic you will not gain a convert to your views and you will probably not keep your friendship!

Neither should you analyse him to his face, unless you want to goad him to fury. Can you imagine the scene?

'You're feeling threatened, aren't you?'

'*Threatened*? Of course not!'

'Well, you tensed up just now, when I said that.'

(Slumping exaggeratedly in his chair and talking loudly) 'No I didn't.'

'Now you're talking loudly. That's another sign of being threatened, you know.'

'I AM NOT FEELING THREATENED.'

'If you weren't you'd be talking normally.'

(Gritting teeth and gripping the arms of his chair, speaking very deliberately and quietly) 'I. Am. Talking. Normally...'

So there's no value in that approach. The only approach that will succeed in the end is...encouragement. Be positive. Agree with what you can. Don't pick up points to battle over. Ask questions. *Listen* to the answers. Gain each other's confidence. It might take a long time. But it will be worth the effort.

So far these examples have featured men. Women are equally in need of reconciliation to others and equally responsive to encouragement. The mannerisms may be different but the underlying needs are the same.

And so far we have considered bringing people *back* together. At the beginning of this chapter we also mentioned how God brings the most unlikely people to work together for the first time, sometimes as man and wife to live together, sometimes to share Christian ministry of a specific kind. And he uses his Barnabases to effect the meetings.

# 'He wants to join us'

Saul of Tarsus was a legend in his day. In this one man were combined an astonishing array of gifts; gifts of race and breeding (he was a privileged Jew), of citizenship (he was born a Roman citizen of the important city of Tarsus in Cilicia, modern Turkey), of standing in his faith (he was a strict Pharisee), of powerful intellect and thorough education. All these gifts he turned to the service of his God. And his one overarching obsession was to rid the land of this upstart sect—'the Way', as they called themselves, the followers of Jesus of Nazareth, the crucified one. They dared to claim that Jesus was the Christ, the Messiah, and that he forgave sins and had risen from the dead. These blasphemies were more than Saul could bear to listen to.

When Stephen, the first Christian martyr, was stoned to death, it was at Saul's feet that the executioners and witnesses laid their clothes.

> *And Saul was there, giving approval to his death*
> (Acts 8:1)

> *Saul began to destroy the church. Going from house to house, he dragged off men and women and put them in prison.*
> (Acts 8:3)

> *Saul was still breathing out murderous threats against the Lord's disciples. He went to the high priest and asked him for letters to the synagogues in Damascus, so that if he found any there who belonged to the Way, whether men or women, he might take them as prisoners to Jerusalem.*
> (Acts 9:1-2)

The young church in Jerusalem was greatly relieved when the persecutor Saul took it into his head to leave for Damascus. For one thing it was a good 150 miles away and it would take him some time to get there and back. And with any luck he might stay there! In fact many days went by and Saul remained absent. The atmosphere in the fellowship eased. Street preaching, caring for the widows, regular worship, all continued in a way which began to seem almost normal.

Then came the bombshell.

'He's back! Saul! Back in Jerusalem! He's been seen! Bolt the doors. Warn the others. Call the committee. He's back.'

So the message sprang from house to house, from street to street, and the church assumed its defensive stance again.

Then came the bigger bombshell.

'He says he's been converted! He claims to have met Jesus

himself. He reckons he was healed from some blindness and baptized by Ananias of Damascus. *He wants to join us!*'

Now it's one thing to pray for someone's conversion but it's quite another to believe it when it happens. Especially if the man concerned is named Saul of Tarsus. So the Jerusalem church met in committee, used their God-given common sense and agreed unanimously that Saul was not really a changed man, that he was probably wishing to plant himself as an agent among them in an outrageous attempt to round them all up in one great and final act of persecution. It was as plain as a pikestaff. People like Saul didn't change overnight.

Unanimously? Not quite. Barnabas had been missing, and only now, at the end of the meeting, did he appear. Men moved to make room for him. He was well liked. When he came into a room everyone felt more relaxed than they had before. And Barnabas looked particularly pleased with himself.

'I am sorry to be so late, but I've been rather busy. And I've got some good news. I have brought a new convert to introduce to you.'

'Barnabas, this is great! Praise the Lord! Anyone you recommend is welcome to join us. Is he here? Bring him in. Introduce him.'

Barnabas paused, as if making the most of a private joke.

'Are you sure, brothers? You won't change your mind? If you don't like my new friend you will have to expel me as well, you know. I am standing surety for him.'

'Don't beat about the bush, Barnabas, bring him in. The poor man's probably wondering what's going on.'

'Very well, brothers. Meet Saul of Tarsus.'

Shocked and horrified silence. Then,

'Barnabas, what *have* you done?'

'We've just made a decision concerning this man. You know how dangerous he is.'

'I know how dangerous he *was*. And I know how dangerous it is for anyone to oppose Jesus Christ...'

*Barnabas took him and brought him to the apostles. He told them how Saul on his journey*

43

*had seen the Lord and that the Lord had spoken
to him, and how in Damascus he had preached
fearlessly in the name of Jesus. So Saul stayed
with them and moved about freely in Jerusalem,
speaking boldly in the name of the Lord.*

(Acts 9:27-28)

# The benefit of the doubt

Barnabas was like that. He had plenty of common sense, like
the rest of them, but he had the gift to see beyond common
sense where necessary. He had taken the trouble to meet Saul
personally, to talk with him at length, to hear his story from
his own lips. He didn't react to 'what they say about Saul',
but he made a relationship—one that was to last for some years
and to the great benefit of the expanding church. He was willing to give Saul the benefit of the doubt.

Within a very short time it must have seemed to Barnabas
that he had made a mistake, however. Saul became so bold
and debated so hotly with the Grecian Jewish party that they
tried to kill him. This time the apostles made a firm decision
and stuck to it. They paid his fare (single) to Tarsus and
escorted him to Caesarea, to make sure he caught his ship.

'Then the church throughout Judea, Galilee and Samaria
enjoyed a time of peace' (Acts 9:31).

Good old Saul! Never a moment's peace when you're around.
Yet surely that's not the end of the story. Retirement among
the dreaming spires of Tarsus is hardly likely to appeal to the
likes of you.

In chapter 7 we shall look in more detail at how Barnabas
introduced Saul again, this time to the church at Antioch where
non-Jews were becoming Christians and the disciples there
earned the most famous nickname in history, 'Christian'. From
there Saul's career as a missionary was fully launched and he
took the new name of Paul. That's another story.

But that story only began because Barnabas was willing to
see the best in someone as unlikely as Saul, willing to talk to
him, to listen to him, no doubt to pray with him, and to build

a bridge, to encourage the apostles to receive him. And what a bridge it was!

---

Is there a 'Saul of Tarsus' who needs to be introduced to your group?
Will you give him/her some of your time? Will you risk the consequences?

---

# 6
# A tragedy in three acts

## Act one: Fairview Avenue

Jane Goodrich balanced the tea tray on her right hand and knocked the bedroom door and opened it simultaneously with her left. Why she knocked the door nobody knew, but her mother always said, 'Come in, dear', as she did every day at precisely 4.45pm when Jane brought the tea. Jane was always in the room before Mrs Goodrich said, 'Come in, dear'.

'I think it's time to draw the blinds, Jane,' said Mrs Goodrich, when the tea tray was fairly settled. She always called the curtains 'the blinds'. Her bed was situated next to the window, which looked out on a stretch of Fairview Avenue. She liked to 'see what was going on', and always enjoyed knowing who was coming to the door before Jane did.

'There's a car just drawn up at number 67,' said Mrs Goodrich, holding back the curtain so that she could see, as she thought, without being seen. 'Whose is it, can you see?' Gina Holwell lived at number 67. Mrs Goodrich always took an interest in her callers. She felt some affinity for her as a widow. 'Can you see?'

'It's a yellow one,' said Jane, not in the least interested. 'I think it's Gordon Barber's. He's probably bringing her the new offerings envelopes or something. Don't worry about him, Mother, your tea-cake will be getting cold.'

Meanwhile Gordon Barber was standing in the hall at number 67. He wasn't delivering offerings envelopes but leaflets for the Sunday School children.

'I hope there'll be enough,' he said. 'You've had a few new ones recently haven't you?'

'Fifteen, sixteen, seventeen,' said Gina. 'Well yes, if they're all there we could use twenty. Is this all they sent?'

'Well no, it wasn't actually,' said Gordon. 'I kept a few back in case the older group wanted them. They said they didn't and I forgot to put them back with these. I'll tell you what. I've got to pass the door tomorrow morning. I'll drop half a dozen in. It'll be quite early. I've got to be at the area conference by nine o'clock. It's an all-day thing, you know. It's just as well Margaret and Shelley are away really. I've got a heap of work to do this evening and I can come and go as I like...No thanks, I'd love a cup, but I must get straight back now...oh yes, they're coming back tomorrow at tea time. I'll meet them at the station. Twenty-four hours is about as much as Granny can stand—Shelley won't stop talking. Well, must go. I'll pop those leaflets in tomorrow. Cheerio.'

He drove off quietly. Too much revving of engines sometimes disturbed Mrs Goodrich.

That was on the Friday evening.

*

At half-past eight the following morning Gordon drew up outside number 67 Fairview Avenue, jumped out of the car without shutting the door, inserted the leaflets in Gina Holwell's letter box and returned to his car. Gina, who had just got up, heard the rattle of the letter box and was in time to unlock the door and wave cheerfully to Gordon as he slammed his car door.

At that precise moment, at number 64, Jane Goodrich opened her mother's curtains.

'Jane dear,' said Mrs Goodrich, 'Mr Barber is just leaving Mrs Holwell's, and she's waving goodbye to him in her dressing gown.'

'Oh Mother, don't be ridiculous,' said Jane, but her eyes told her that her mother was speaking the truth. 'Anyway, there must be some simple explanation. He's probably just called back.'

'I didn't hear his car door,' said Mrs Goodrich firmly, 'and she was in her dressing gown.'

'Well, it's no business of ours, is it?' said Jane, confused. Her mother didn't like her involvement at the church and was always ready to criticize its members.

'It might be, dear,' said Mrs Goodrich solemnly. 'I think you ought to make a few enquiries, just to be quite sure, you know. We don't want a scandal to break out in Fairview Avenue, do we?'

For ninety-five years old and at 8.35 a.m. on a Saturday, Jane thought, her mother was remarkably alert. She had not, purposefully not, mentioned the possibility of a scandal at the church.

# Act two: Food Fayre

Later that Saturday morning, Jane Goodrich was trying to concentrate on her shopping. But she kept forgetting where she had put her list and wondering about Gordon Barber and Gina Holwell. *Surely* not. It was impossible! But Gina was a widow, not all that merry of course, but she did live alone, and that cheery goodbye wave, and the dressing gown...

Vivien James was doubtfully picking up tomatoes and putting them down again.

'Hello, Vivien,' said Jane. 'How are you?'

'I'm fine, thanks. And you? And your mother? Is she all right? Oh good. I *must* come round and see her some time. I know she likes a change of company...oh dear, how dreadful! I didn't mean that she's bored with you, you know. I mean it must be good for her to see more people. I hope you're not offended?'

Jane laughed for the first time that day. Perhaps at *last*, someone would come and break their monotony. 'No, of course not,' she said. 'Come whenever you like. When can Walter spare you?'

'Oh, he's all right. He can look after himself for an hour or two. These men aren't as helpless as they seem, you know. Gordon's managing perfectly well without Margaret, I'm sure...'

Vivien was saying something else, but Jane's world had tilted sideways and she held up her hand. 'What did you say? Is Margaret away?'

'Just for the night, yes. She's taken little Shelley to see her Granny. It was her birthday I think. And Shelley loves to stay the night. It's half-term you see, so Shelley has Friday and Monday. It's an odd arrangement that...'

'Vivien,' Jane interrupted, her voice trembling, 'there's something you ought to know. I don't know who else to tell and I must share it with someone. For your prayers.'

Jane recounted her fears to Vivien. Vivien could hardly believe it, but the facts were pretty stubborn-looking.

'Don't spread it round. It's too dreadful. But I suppose I'd better go and see Timothy.'

So Vivien went home in a very worried frame of mind and told Walter all about it, so that he too could pray. Jane called on Timothy Monteith (who had hoped to have a day off because there weren't any weddings) and told him all about it. He assured her that there could be nothing in it, but he told Diana, his wife, and they both prayed about it...

By the end of Saturday thirteen people were informed so that they could pray about it and another fifteen, who had no intention of praying at all, were rather gleefully informing each other of the 'facts' as they were known.

Meanwhile Gordon met Margaret and Shelley and heard all

about Granny's new cat, and Gina Holwell spent a pleasant evening with her sister, several miles away. These four at least were blissfully unaware of the scandal.

## Act three: Sunday morning

The children from the Sunday School join the rest of the congregation after the sermon. Shelley appears with the rest, clutching today's piece of original artwork, and sits by her mother. The seat beside Gordon is vacant. One hundred and six pairs of eyes stray over the tops of their hymn books to see who will occupy the seat next to Gordon (*Joy of heav'n to earth come down*). Surely not, in full view of the *whole* church? (*All thy faithful mercies crown*). Yes. Gina Holwell. (*Pure unbounded love thou art*). How *blatant* can you get? (*Enter ev'ry trembling heart*). She must be totally insensitive! (*Let us all thy life receive*). And he's sharing his hymn book with her! (*Never more thy temples leave*). And there's Margaret not seeming to mind or to notice. (*Thee we would be always blessing, serve thee as thy hosts above...*).

## Gossip, the enemy of encouragement

Fortunately that particular 'scandal' was easily defused, but it left behind some painful memories. Timothy asked Gordon, in a fairly offhand way, about his visit to Gina, and very soon discovered the truth of the matter. Gordon was at first highly amused and then, as the implications began to dawn on him, very angry, and later extremely sad. Although the whole scandal only lasted for a few days, it took a very long time for the effects to go away.

Gordon and Margaret felt very hurt and so did Gina. Vivien and particularly Jane felt guilty for spreading a lie, but how could they have known? What *ought* Jane to have done? Mrs Goodrich remained unrepentant and would only say, you never really *knew*, did you?

Many were saddened by the affair but many others were secretly disappointed that there had been no real scandal at all.

50

Why is scandal so attractive? Why is gossip so prevalent, in Christian fellowships where it ought to be totally outlawed, as well as in less high-minded circles?

For one thing, people are always interested in people, what they look like, what they are doing, why they do it. The huge following commanded by TV soap opera bears witness to this fact. We get fascinated by a character and we want to know what happens next. We either identify with the character and hope they come out on top, or we conceive a dislike for someone and delight when they get their come-uppance.

These attitudes spill over into real life too. However experienced we are as Christians there is a terrible temptation to delight in someone else's downfall, to be secretly pleased when he or she bites the dust.

Then, of course, there's the pleasure of knowing something that the other person doesn't know, the secret which has reached *me* but has yet to reach *you* and I am the privileged one who is about to bestow my knowledge on you. It gives me a feeling of superiority, to be the one 'in the know' who is informing the rest.

But why do we, who profess to live by the love of Christ and in the power of the Holy Spirit, have these temptations to be gleeful when someone else is in trouble? And why discuss such a painful subject when we thought we were concentrating on encouragement?

To answer the second question first, gossip is the opposite of encouragement. It is one of the most *dis*couraging aspects of much church life and needs to be denounced as the evil thing it is. All those excuses: 'I *must* tell someone', 'Just for your prayer', 'Timothy needs to know of course'... If we really mean to be encouraging and to practise the ministry of encouragement, gossip must be very firmly put aside. Encouragement is hard to spread. Gossip is as contagious as a forest fire.

*If you have any encouragement from being united*
*with Christ, if any comfort from his love, if any*
*fellowship with the Spirit, if any tenderness and*

51

*compassion, then make my joy complete by being*
*like-minded, having the same love, being one in*
*spirit and purpose.*

(Philippians 2:1-2)

If we really love someone can we spread evil rumours about them?

Why *do* we do it?

It is probably because of our own sense of insecurity. If we can denigrate others then we hope to rise in the esteem of our hearers by comparison. Instead of praising others (and running the risk of appearing insipid beside them) we delight in criticizing them ('for their own good' of course!) or making jokes about them. Sarcasm is the easiest form of character-assassination and the most despicable. We are jealous. We wish to appear better than we are, to shine in public esteem, so we tarnish the others in the vain hope that our synthetic gleam will be noticed. In fact, of course, we tarnish ourselves much more than the others.

But gossip *is* contagious and if we do it, others will find an excuse for doing it too. And if they do it, we make ourselves more comfortable about it. It is a devilish spiral, and the Father of Lies down below must chuckle mightily when he sees it.

# 'Mud thrown is ground lost'

Among the quotations, cartoons, postcards and other pieces of paper on my office wall is a card bearing a picture of a castaway on a *very* small island (about six feet square). He is surrounded not only by water but by numbers of hungry-looking alligators. He is busily engaged in hurling great chunks of the island at the alligators. His island is rapidly disappearing.

The caption reads, 'Mud thrown is ground lost'.

In few places can this be more true than in the Christian church, a church deeply in need of encouragement and building up. The discouragement of negativity, criticism and gossip is a tragedy.

But enough tragedy. Let's move on to see how Barnabas

put new life into people by affirming, promoting and encouraging them.

Check on that story you are tempted to 'share':
   Is it true?
   Is it kind?
   Is it going to build up the church?
If you answer 'no' or 'don't know' to any of these questions then don't spread it round.

# 7
# Surgery

**B**arnabas was one of those rare people who can spot gifts in others and bring them into the centre of the stage without intruding themselves. He would be glad to see Saul being interviewed on television without himself appearing at the corner of the picture and mouthing 'Hello Mother' at the camera.

Such people are rare because the shy and retiring among us don't usually promote other people, and the competitors among us are jealous of the success of others, so even try to hold them back. Even in the church? Even in the church. And encouraging people can be a very painful process.

# The one-man band

Timothy sat in his study, staring gloomily at the wall. He felt utterly trapped. It seemed to him that one half of his congregation wanted him to take the lead in everything, to display all known gifts and a few more besides and generally to act like a one-man band. The other half seemed to be in rebellion against him, claiming that they had all the gifts needed to run the church and hinting that they could very well do without him. Neither side was encouraging him. The one was trying to bury him under intolerable pressure, the other trying to ignore him altogether.

Yet he had a clear idea of what he was there for. He believed that God had called him to the ministry and specifically to be vicar of Canwell Park. His task was not to dominate the church as if it was his church: it was God's church. He could not possibly come up to the standard required by some: to be 'good with the elderly', 'good with the children', 'good with the youth', a brilliant preacher, an understanding counsellor, a superb chairman of committees, an indefatigable parish visitor, a model husband and father, a man of great learning who should spend his time in his study, a 'man of the people' who ought to be in the pub where the men are, a good social mixer, a local politician...

He jerked upright in his chair and emerged from the nightmare into which he was sliding. On the other hand, was he supposed to sit back and do nothing and watch the church...do what? According to one group, it would grow in the Spirit if Timothy stopped interfering. The other group feared that it would fall into even more chaos if he didn't 'take a firm line' (whatever that was supposed to mean). In practice it would probably result in open warfare between the two groups.

Surely his task was to be the conductor of the orchestra, calling out the gifts of each of the players, not making the music himself but overseeing the pattern of church life so that it made a harmony which was pleasing to God.

That was a positive thought anyway. He wrote it down and

let it sink into his mind and his imagination for a luxurious twenty minutes.

# Three in a row

'Hello. Hello. Mrs Morrison? How are you? Good, and your husband?...Yes. I suppose he is...Yes, it was Gavin I wanted to speak to actually. Is he in? He won't mind if I interrupt his homework for a minute or two?...'

'Hello Gavin. Sorry to drag you from your work. I'm 'phoning to ask whether you can do a little job for me—well, not for me but for Mr and Mrs Staindrop. You know Mrs Staindrop, her husband brings her to church in a wheelchair. Is it possible for you to spend an hour a week tidying their garden for them—choose any day? It'll be sweeping up leaves now and then and cutting out some jungle at first, but there'd be more to do in the spring of course, when the grass begins to grow. Old Bert can't do it now...

'Thanks, Gavin, that would be a great help. I'll leave you to make the arrangement. I mentioned your name when I was round there earlier today and she said, "Oh yes, that nice young gentleman who brought me a cup of coffee one Sunday." So you've made a hit there.'

Timothy put down the receiver and drew a neat line through one of the items on his 'things-to-do' list. He paused, and picked up the 'phone again:

'Bob? Hello Bob, how are you? I'm well thanks, yes...What can you do for me, well, not so much for me but for the church, perhaps I should say for the Lord. Does that sound pious?...yes, I should have known better than to ask you that, shouldn't I? Anyway, I think we should extend the number of people who lead the intercessions in the morning service—the prayer time—and I think you would do it really well. Would you like to have a go this Sunday? Good, I thought you would. Between five and ten minutes, certainly no more than ten. Fine. Thank you so much, goodbye.'

Timothy drew another neat line on his list, paused again and found Gordon Barber's number.

The 'phone rang at number 34 Highwood Avenue just as Margaret was opening the oven door and Gordon was scrambling into the loft, looking for an old pair of boots that he remembered putting up in the roof last winter. The 'phone stopped ringing abruptly.

'Hello. 5742. This is Shelley Barber speaking. Can I help you?'

Gordon and Margaret, from different ends of the house, felt a glow of pride that their little Shelley should be answering the 'phone so beautifully. She'd make a very efficient secretary one of these days.

'Oh, it's you, Timothy.'

Margaret dropped the grill pan on the floor. How many times have I told her not to call the Vicar by his Christian name?

'Yes, he is in. He's very well. Well, he's a bit silly sometimes!' Her sentence ended in a stifled giggle.

'He had to cook for himself because Mummy and me went to Granny's and he forgot the potatoes; and the water boiled away and the potatoes burnt all black...yes, he *was*, wasn't he?'

Gordon was finding this conversation, or the end he could hear, very disquieting so he went and stood firmly in front of Shelley. She waved him away and turned her back on him.

'But he did go and love old Mr Kent when I told him to, so he's not so bad really, is he?...Of course I do, he's my daddy...Yes, thanks, we had a lovely time. Granny took me to see Father Christmas. He wasn't the real one—the real one doesn't come until Christmas. I think this one is his assistant, you know. He was quite nice but he smelt a bit funny...yes... yes...bye bye.'

'Shelley, you impossible child!' burst out Gordon. 'Didn't he want to talk to me or to Mummy?'

'No,' said Shelley firmly. 'He wanted to talk to me.'

'But didn't he ask whether I was here?'

'Yes, he did. And I told him you were. He's very interested in Granny and in Father Christmas. He agrees with me that the man we saw was Father Christmas's assistant.'

Shelley walked solemnly away, and Gordon made for the 'phone.

'Timothy, please forgive my daughter. She got to the 'phone before I could.'

'Don't apologize, Gordon—I enjoyed that little talk better than any I've had for a long time. And it was the third encouraging 'phone call in a row...'

# The fifth call

'Four in a row.' Timothy drew another line. 'Two for the price of one at the Barbers'. That Shelley will go far. Darling I've just been speaking to Shelley Barber. "Can I help you?" she said, and, "Oh, it's you, Timothy", and, "Daddy's a bit silly sometimes", and the best of all, the man she saw in the department store was Father Christmas's assistant. "One of his assistants, you know." She's priceless!'

Diana handed him a cup of tea. 'How are you getting on, dear?'

'Fine, fine. Just one more call and I'll call it a day. Sorry, no joke intended. I've had four good positive calls in a row. It makes a change.'

Without pausing he picked up the receiver again.

'Jane, Timothy here...Yes, I'm fine thank you. And how's mother? She really is wonderful, you know, at her age—she's very alert. Doesn't miss a thing...'

Jane has registered three messages so far; the Vicar has asked after her mother but has not stopped to ask after *her*. He has said what they all say, 'What a wonderful old lady your mother is!' when the wonderful old lady does nothing but *sit* there all day and *lie* there all night and I'm the one who does all the work. But I'm not wonderful. I'm just a movable piece of furniture. *And* he naively noticed that she doesn't miss a thing. She doesn't indeed. It was her nosiness that started that awful Gina Holwell-Gordon Barber business...

Hurt feelings prompt quick thinking. But Timothy is still talking:

'I've been thinking that you have so much to do, looking after your mother and so on' (good, he has noticed) 'and I realize that you're not as young as you used to be either' (that's

58

a nasty one, what's he getting at?) 'so I thought that you'd be pleased to know that we shan't expect you to stand for re-election for the church council next year.'

There was a long silence while Jane fought back the tears. He didn't know, perhaps he couldn't know, how much she valued that one chance to be of use, to get away from this bedroom for one evening every six weeks, to feel part of the church, to feel that she *mattered*. She gave up the struggle, burst into tears and slammed down the receiver.

Timothy was stunned. Most of the members of the church council would love to be given their freedom, he supposed. What an odd response! He must have misjudged her. Oh well, another visit tomorrow! Encouraging people could be exciting and rewarding but it was very painful when it went wrong.

He thoughtfully put a ring round the name of Goodrich on his list, instead of crossing it out.

# Gilbert and Sullivan

Barnabas's reputation in the Jerusalem church was dented by the Saul of Tarsus affair. The man he'd backed and pinned his hopes on had let him down rather. Certainly Saul had demonstrated that he really *was* a new man. Christ really had stopped him in his tracks and made him long to preach the good news instead of defying the man who claimed to be the Son of God.

But Saul really had been unwise. Much too outspoken. No tact at all, yet he was so obviously gifted and his new faith was so real. Surely Saul had a future in the church. He couldn't just retire to Tarsus...

Some time later, Barnabas was sent by the church in Jerusalem to oversee an important new work of God in the great city of Antioch in northern Syria. 'A great number of people were brought to the Lord', says Luke, the author of Acts, and Barnabas saw his big chance. He was well clear of Jerusalem and the people who feared Saul. In fact Antioch and Tarsus were only a few days' journey apart, over a hundred miles round the top right-hand corner of the Mediterranean perhaps, but a short distance to accomplish what Barnabas had in mind:

> *Then Barnabas went to Tarsus to look for Saul, and when he found him, he brought him to Antioch. So for a whole year Barnabas and Saul met with the church and taught great numbers of people. The disciples were first called Christians at Antioch.*
>
> (Acts 11:25-26)

Barnabas took Saul with him to Jerusalem again soon afterwards. The occasion was the first ever Christian Aid collection for the famine-stricken church in Judaea. The Antioch collection was taken by Barnabas and Saul on the long 300 mile journey. They got there without being robbed and accomplished their mission. They could ill afford to stay long in Jerusalem, but while they were there they must have painted a glowing picture of Christian life in Antioch because young John Mark volunteered to go with them. Perhaps Barnabas liked the look of him. Here was someone else to encourage into service (Acts 11:27-30; 12:25).

There followed one of the most dramatic stories of missionary endeavour to have come down to us from the infant church. Saul and Barnabas were sent out with the blessing of the church at Antioch and by the express command of the Spirit of God, into Asia Minor, on what was to be known as Paul's first missionary journey. New churches sprang to life in the path of the disciples—not just Paul (who seems to have got his new name in Cyprus during this journey) but Barnabas *and* John Mark (Acts 13:5). But Mark left them on their return to the mainland (13:13) and returned to Jerusalem.

The missionary tour was a triumph and Paul and Barnabas were seen as a great two-man team, their names ever linked like a spiritual Gilbert and Sullivan. They represented Antioch in the Great Council of Jerusalem when it was agreed that non-Jews might be allowed equal status with Jews as Christians, and they returned and taught in Antioch for another period of great encouragement (Acts 15:1-35). John Mark must also have returned to Antioch by this time. Considering the lack of public transport, these people certainly did get about!

Paul decided to do the missionary tour again, to encourage the young churches. Barnabas was enthusiastic. Here was a chance to meet old friends and encourage them *and* to give John Mark the chance to get more experience. But Paul said 'no'. Barnabas was stunned. Young John Mark had a great future. But Paul was adamant. If he'd left them once he'd leave them again.

The Gilbert and Sullivan partnership broke up in a quarrel over a carpet in the Savoy Theatre. Barnabas and Paul parted over the suitability of John Mark to go with them. Gilbert and Sullivan were professional entertainers. Barnabas and Paul were effectively professional Christians, but 'they had such a sharp disagreement that they parted company. Barnabas took Mark and sailed for Cyprus, but Paul chose Silas and...went through Syria and Cilicia, strengthening the churches' (Acts 15:39-41).

Who was right? Who knows? We do know that Paul in later life found John Mark a great help: 'Get Mark and bring him with you, because he is helpful to me in my ministry' (2 Timothy 4:11). What a tragedy that the pain of separation should have been sharpened by a quarrel, a 'sharp disagreement'.

Barnabas had set about talent-spotting. He had acted as Paul's agent, introducing him to the Jerusalem church and rescuing him from obscurity in Tarsus. He had accompanied him for many weary and dangerous miles and been willing to become Paul's number two (at Lystra the people noted that Paul was the chief speaker). Barnabas risked, and lost, their friendship when he refused to abandon John Mark.

A simple but painful truth emerges. Encouragement, the promotion of others, is a vital and rewarding task, but it can, and will, be acutely painful too. The encourager is called to suffer pain.

But the pain is not all negative. It is the pain of putting heart into others. Open-heart surgery is always painful.

Promoting others always apparently involves a decrease in one's own standing.
Does encouraging always *have* to involve pain for the encourager or the encouraged?

# 8
# The sharp edge

Encouragement sometimes hurts. This happens not only when the encouragers are clumsy and get it wrong, nor even when the person being encouraged misses the point and takes it badly. Sometimes encouragement *needs* to hurt. It is no rope of wool which feels soft and warm but which parts whenever weight is put on it. It is composed of strong fibres which can take the strain—and sometimes they scratch.

That spectacular eleventh-century strip-cartoon, commonly known as the Bayeux Tapestry, describes the political and military doings of Duke William of Normandy. It also pictures in superb detail many of the happenings of everyday life which would otherwise have been lost to us.

In one scene, towards the end of the Battle of Hastings, we meet Bishop Odo, riding near to the Duke. The Bishop is distinguished by his coat of bright red armour (perhaps a kind of 'Red Cross' indicating, 'don't kill me, I'm a bishop. I'm unarmed'). Whether he should have been in a battle at all is a debatable point, but at least he has kept the rules to the

letter. He is not carrying a sword. His claim is therefore that he is unarmed. He is nevertheless to be seen brandishing a very heavy stick ('BACULU TENENS', as the blurb helpfully remarks), which looks like a baseball bat with knobs on it.

He appears to be aiming a vigorous blow at a soldier who is passing him, going in the opposite direction. One of the

Saxons who has penetrated the Norman lines, perhaps? But no. Again the commentary tells us what is going on: 'Here Bishop Odo, brandishing his staff, comforts the troops.' The words are 'CONFORTAT PUEROS', literally, 'strengthens the lads'.

Comfort here has its old meaning, 'putting power with', '*for-ti*fying'—nothing to do with slippers by the fire or putting an arm round the shoulders. It is clear that the unfortunate target of the Bishop's wrath is one of his own men, caught in the act of running away (or perhaps, to be more generous to the poor man, unable to control his horse, who is running away). The episcopal blessing arrives in the form of a vigorous blow on top of the helmet from a big stick. He is comforted, and, no doubt, were the cartoon to be animated, we should see him turning round and joining his Duke and his Bishop in the victory which is about to take place.

All this brings clearly into focus the meaning of the word 'comfort', very closely akin to encouragement. For the English word 'encourage' means 'make courageous' or 'put heart into'. It is not a matter of being stroked or patted on the head, but beefed up into action.

# Confrontation

To be encouraged or comforted in this rather violent way is neither English nor pleasant, but it is frequently nearer to the biblical meaning of encouragement than our usual soft notion.

When King David found himself at one of the lower points in his switchback career, when he came to Ziklag and discovered the town to be a smoking ruin with wives and sons and daughters taken captive, he and his men 'wept aloud until they had no strength left to weep' (1 Samuel 30:4). His own men threatened to stone him to death. At that absolute low point, David 'encouraged himself in the Lord', as the King James Version has it. 'He *found strength* in the LORD his God' (NIV verse 6). He prayed, took 400 of his best men, pursued the Amalekite raiders and rescued the families and possessions intact. That's encouragement at work!

What about Barnabas? Did he always make it soft for Paul? Obviously not, as we saw in the last chapter. In Acts 15:36-41 he confronted Paul over the John Mark question. His encouragement of Paul was not fawning or soft. Neither did he wish to spite Paul—at least, there is no obvious reason why he should. No, he felt sure that Mark needed affirming and strengthening and perhaps that Paul would be stronger if someone stood up to him. As we shall see later, it seems that they went too far in their expression of their respective points of view. It was certainly vigorous!

But this uncomfortable comfort does not even stop here. American author Gordon MacDonald, with his wife, Gail, has written a booklet with the title *Affirmation and Rebuke*. Affirmation is positive encouragement. Rebuke is much nearer to a buffet from Bishop Odo of Bayeux. But it is part of God's way of dealing with his people and we need to be wise enough and strong enough to employ rebuke, in a humble fashion, when it is called for. Confrontation is sometimes necessary, either to clear the air and mend a broken relationship or to get someone on the road of encouragement - a good sharp push to get them going.

Dandelions are one of the gardener's enemies. Their strident yellow heads clash with other flowers which the gardener intends to be there and they break up the smooth green turf of a well-behaved lawn. Superficially, of course, it's easy to rid the garden of dandelions. The stalks are brittle, the leaves tear easily. Just grab them up in handfuls. Within a week or two they are all back in their former profusion. The dandelion root is long and strong and rarely does it come up with a simple tug on the surface. It needs to be dug out. It requires confrontation, a painful business for both gardener and, one might guess, for the dandelion. For the encouragement of the garden, painful confrontation is necessary. This can also apply to our ministry of encouragement.

A very serious double difficulty presents itself at this point. Most of us prefer to avoid conflict if we can, and this avoidance is fortified by Christian principles. 'Love your neighbour as yourself' is often interpreted to mean, 'don't rock the boat', 'do nothing to upset anyone', and so many of us who need kindly but firm confrontation, a gentle but clear rebuke or even vigorous discipline, never get it because our friends are afraid to upset us. We too draw back from offending them, and hurts remain unhealed, pain is driven below the surface, grudges are harboured, gossip begins and the body of Christ is torn with unnecessary injury.

The other side of this double difficulty is the excessive readiness of some to be always confronting, complaining and berating others, especially clergy and ministers, who are constantly a target for this kind of barrage. As a result they grow thick skins to avoid severe emotional damage, and real problems that need to be dealt with are turned aside along with the rest of the tirade.

The meek and mild person, however, takes a great deal of insult and injury without saying a word. Some people's capacity for absorbing pain verbally and emotionally is astonishing. But there may well come that final straw, that last sharp word or being ignored for the hundredth time, which builds up the pressure too far. The retaining walls collapse and a flood of imprisoned anger and repressed resentment is released with a power that often astonishes the aggrieved person as well as the target of the deluge.

This may result in a healthy 'clearing of the air', a commitment to listen quietly to each other and mend the relationship, but it is equally likely to cause deeper damage. The fury of the onslaught is very hard for the object to bear. He or she usually becomes defensive rather than amenable. What is being said is often exaggerated: 'you *always*', 'you *never*', '*every*one says so', and the frequent response to this kind of generalized anger is a loss of temper on both sides. 'Why didn't you tell me before?'; 'Why couldn't you have taken these problems one at a time as they occurred, instead of letting them build up such a head of steam?'

The essence of this difficulty is that the aggrieved person has attacked the other from a sense of his own frustration—not with the purpose of building up and encouraging. This is usually destructive when it is allowed to build up to such a pitch. The difficult path, but one which is necessary, is the path of confronting for the good, benefit and encouragement of the other, rather than the necessity of 'blowing one's top'.

# Timothy confronted

Jane Goodrich had plenty of time to revolve such thoughts in her mind the day following her 'phone conversation with the vicar. Initially she had been furious. How could anyone be so unfeeling and thoughtless as to insult her in such a way? Didn't her feelings matter? Was she not supposed to have any? And *he* calls himself a minister of God! Don't they train you to be sensitive in theological colleges? Doesn't experience of ministry show you how people feel?

These were Jane's confused thoughts as she tried without much success to sleep. By the next morning her emotions had cooled sufficiently for some reflective thought. It was clear that she needed to discuss this problem with someone. *Not* her mother! Jane continued to keep up her accustomed flow of patter and believed that her mother had not noticed that anything was wrong. It would be better not to spread the problem around. She had learned that from the Gina Holwell affair. No, she must see Timothy, perhaps Timothy and Diana together. But she was obviously not in a fit state to see him yet. Her 'composure' this morning was largely the result of lack of sleep and she knew that, if the surface were scratched, a fresh violent explosion would result.

It occurred to her at this point that prayer would be appropriate. How dreadful! Twelve (mostly) wakeful hours of emotional turmoil and she had not attempted to discuss the matter with her Lord! Was she not a disciple of Christ, and did she not tell people like Vivien James to claim the full citizenship of the kingdom of heaven that is theirs, and here was she, in great need of strength and comfort, having *forgotten* to pray...

She spent a considerable part of the rest of the morning before an open Bible, and after a great deal of heart-searching assured herself that her place on the church council was not really the problem at all— what mattered was whether she was valued as a person in her own right— and what mattered for the church was that its minister should be helped to *see* that people mattered. She decided that it was not condescending on her part to conclude that he needed more help than she did. She would wait for a day or so, to be quite sure that her anger would not dominate events, and then ask to see Timothy and Diana.

Meanwhile back at the vicarage, Timothy rather guiltily crossed out the name of Jane Goodrich from his list of things to do today and entered it under 'tomorrow'. He had a sermon to prepare and so many other things to do and he couldn't face a tearful middle-aged lady today. So it was the day following that Jane's 'phone rang and she found herself being invited to tea with Timothy and Diana. Progress was imminent.

The details of that long conversation are personal and confidential. Some tears were shed. All three learned more about themselves, each other and God than they would have thought possible. Each had come prepared to hear the truth and prepared to tell the truth as they saw it. It was a very encouraging meeting for them all, and it had further repercussions on the rest of the church. The sharp edge had cut deeply.

---

Encouragement, putting new heart into someone, strengthening them, beefing them up, can be painful for both parties. Are we prepared to suffer that pain? Are we prepared, under God, to *inflict* it where necessary?

---

# 9

# Listen!

The Gina Holwell/Gordon Barber 'scandal' had at least two effects, one predictable, the other unexpected. The first was that Gina and Jane started avoiding each other. Each felt that they should make a move towards the other. Both put it off until it became more and more difficult to see how they could break the ice again. This was all the more embarrassing because they lived opposite each other, and hard to reconcile with being in church together, especially at communion services.

The unexpected result was that Gina and Margaret Barber quite suddenly became friends. After the gossip and excitement had been laid to rest, Gordon and Margaret had asked

Gina over for supper and spent a relaxed evening together. The Barbers had never met this side of Gina before. They had known her as wound up like a spring, sharp, over-busy and always having an answer for everything. They had encouraged her to talk about Andrew, her late husband. She had never spoken of him. It was as if she had blotted him out of her conscious mind, his death had been such a painful blow, and her tautness was the result. Talking about Andrew seemed to ease the tension.

Freed from being bombarded by Gina's demands for her to have more faith and trust the Bible, Margaret was able to find that they had quite a bit in common, especially as she gingerly shared her fear of losing Gordon— one of her greatest worries. Here was someone whose worst fears had been realized. Andrew really had died in a road accident in fog. Surely this of all possible topics of conversation would be the most painful. Gordon was quick to see that it might be a very beneficial encounter, so he slipped off to see whether Shelley needed a glass of water.

Gina went home in a reflective state of mind. She and Margaret had seemed to be so far apart: herself confident and full of faith, at least full of answers to people's problems; Margaret so full of doubts and negative responses. Yet both of them had started at the same point—they feared to lose their security, their husbands. She had lost hers and had responded by becoming hard and tense. Margaret had not lost her husband but her fear had pushed her in the opposite direction, into confusion and doubt, even concerning the basic facts of Christianity, even of the existence of God. She could believe in her head, but the belief had not made the short journey to her heart. Gina switched off her car's engine and determined to discover more about Margaret Barber. She closed the garage door as quietly as she could and smiled grimly as she saw the edge of Mrs Goodrich's curtain fall back into place. The light was always on all night. Did she ever sleep?

72

# Are doubts just bad luck?

The next time Gina met Margaret Gordon was out and they had time to talk.

'Margaret, I owe you an apology.'

'What for?'

'For spending so much time telling you what I thought you ought to do or think or believe. You helped me last week, you know. You made me realize something I'd never noticed before. I've been trying to cover up my feelings about Andrew and it's come out in trying to make people see things exactly as I do. I'm trying now not to force other people to believe the same. It's quite a relief really. Does this make sense to you?'

'You make a lot of sense, Gina. And you're much easier to talk to. Do you know, I used to try to avoid meeting you in case you gave me a lecture!'

'Margaret, how *awful*! But I can see how it happened. And I've realized that we both have exactly the same problem, fear of insecurity, and it takes you one way and me in exactly the opposite way. We are so alike in needs and so different in the way we react, that we have got across one another.'

Margaret laughed. 'I expect you're right,' she said. 'But how much of all that would have come out if you hadn't been on that pastoral counselling course? It all sounds a bit psychological to me, and that's one of my difficulties. It, I mean this question of faith, can all be explained by psychologists. We've discussed it before so I won't start it all over again. But now you seem to be saying that faith is only *your* response to insecurity and *my* response to the same problem is *un*faith. Bad luck me!'

Gina was silent for a few moments. Margaret half expected the usual barrage of answers to her problem. Instead, Gina said quietly:

'Do you think it's just bad luck that you have doubts?'

'Yes, I suppose I do. It seems so easy for some people. Like you, for instance. I just seem to have been blessed, or should I say cursed, with the kind of mind that sees everything in its worst light. If someone tells me something, I find a small voice inside me saying, "What if it's not true?" The more sure people are of things, the louder the voice. And I suppose I've been given a mind that's able to think about things and there always seems to be another side to every idea. Some very intelligent and eminent people have a firm belief in God, but that doesn't prove anything. Other equally impressive people are convinced atheists.

'I know all the arguments. I can recite the evidences for the resurrection and I can't honestly come to any other conclusion than that it happened—it all fits together. But then the voice says, "You can't be *sure*, can you?" And I say, "No, I can't." It always comes round to that.

'Now I know the next thing you're going to say. Your counselling course will have told you that I must have had some bad experience as a child, perhaps even at birth, which has blocked off my ability to be positive about anything. The little voice is really something repressed in my past which is poisoning the present. Well, I've been all through that one and I can find nothing that could possibly have that effect. I've been prayed for and prayed with and prayed over and prayed through.

'Some people have said it must be something occult. But I've never had anything to do with the occult. I don't think I've ever read a horoscope! I've had prayer and deliverance for that too, just in case.'

There was a silence, but not an uncomfortable silence.

'You've really been through the mill, haven't you?' said Gina at length.

'I think I have.'

'And it's all due to bad luck? There's nothing you can do about it?'

'Nothing.'

'So I have the ability to choose to believe and you haven't?'

'It looks like that, doesn't it?'

'But is it like that really, Margaret? Do you *have* to obey this small voice? Are you prepared to let it ruin your life?'

'Yes,' said Margaret in a small voice, 'I suppose I am. I've just said so, haven't I?'

'Are you an adult, Margaret?'

'Of course I am. What are you getting at?'

'Well, if you are, you have to take the responsibility of making adult decisions. They may be painful, but they're up to you. Next time you hear that small voice, listen to it politely and then quite deliberately and firmly decide whether you accept what it says or not.'

'But what if I'm wrong?'

'What if you are? A mistake isn't everything. The important thing is that you will have taken charge in a grown up way and decided something. I think you will improve with practice.'

# Barnabas the listener?

Was Barnabas a good listener? He is nowhere described as such, but there are a few clues. For one thing it is very difficult to imagine anyone being good at encouragement who is *not* a good listener. Encouragement is not constantly talking to people, even when you're giving them good reasons to be encouraged. Encouragement is also a matter of accepting people as they are and receiving them at their face value. And there's no better way of affirming someone than to listen to them attentively. Many people who experience being listened to carefully and attentively for even five minutes, without interruption, are amazed at the effect it has on them. 'I never realized anyone cared about me before', 'I matter enough for you to listen to *me*'. It's a powerful and all too rare experience.

Then again, Barnabas seems to have been the only member of the church in Jerusalem who listened to Saul of Tarsus. The other believers were panic-stricken at his appearance, when he claimed to have been converted (see page 43), but it was Barnabas who 'told them how Saul on his journey had seen the Lord and that the Lord had spoken to him, and how in Damascus he had preached fearlessly in the name of Jesus' (Acts 9:27). Barnabas must have been doing some careful listening. He was able to repeat it all in detail too, which shows that he had paid attention.

Another hint may be gleaned from the experience of Paul and Barnabas at Lystra (Acts 14:8-20). The superstitious inhabitants imagined that the gods had come down to earth in human form. 'Barnabas they called Zeus, and Paul they called Hermes because he was the chief speaker' (verse 12). Hermes, or Mercury, was the messenger of the gods in classical mythology. He did the talking. Paul filled the role admirably. Zeus, or Jupiter, was the king of the gods. Barnabas appeared to them as the strong and silent one. Paul spoke, Barnabas listened. This may be an unfair inference of course, but it fits in with what we already know about him.

## Learning to listen

Whether we have assessed Barnabas' listening skill correctly or not, it is clear that Gina's new approach to Margaret was far better than her previous hectoring, lecturing and haranguing. She was learning to listen, and Margaret, as a result, was learning to listen to herself. No longer did she have to defend herself against the onslaught. Gradually, gently she was being drawn out, to step back and see herself more as she really was.

Learning to listen is not easy, yet it is, as we have seen, a vital ingredient in encouragement. It requires a determined effort of concentration. We are all too familiar with the frustration of the conversation that goes thus:

A: 'How are you?'

You: 'Not too bad.'

A: 'That sounds as if you are not too good. Is something the matter?' (This sounds promising. You have hoped to find someone who is interested enough to let you unburden yourself.)

You: 'Well, I've had some problems with lack of sleep...'

A: 'You *have*? So have I. What a coincidence! Sometimes it's three in the morning before I can get off and I always wake at six. You know, *I* think it's something in the water...'

A is listening only to A, not to you at all. Sometimes people who have learned a bit about listening, like Gina they have been on counselling courses, are able to school themselves to listen to the end of your side of the conversation. You can tell that they are affirming you, looking at you, not out of the window, paying attention with all their might, yet even then they are so anxious to tell you about their own experience that you wonder whether they were really *with* you in the first place. Gina Holwell had learned some techniques, but she only began to learn to listen to the *person* when she became involved with Margaret.

There is one simple point, simple but very difficult to achieve. I am at the centre of my life. You are at the centre of yours. My experiences are so important to me that I assume that they will be of equal interest and importance to you. So I 'listen' to what you say with as much concentration as I can muster, while secretly waiting for the chance to present you with what is in my mind, *my* experience. In other words, I'm not really listening to *you* at all.

I fear that if there is a silence after you have spoken, we may lose the thread of conversation. I am quite sure that my words of wisdom will help you. In both cases I am probably wrong. A short silence can be of great value in allowing your friend's thoughts to be reflected back, to be able to speak to him/herself. And to enable the Holy Spirit to speak. Where do we leave enough space for God to get a word in edgeways?

So the simple point is this: When your friend pauses for breath, wait for more. If there is a silence, preserve it for a few moments. Then ask whether there is anything else they would like to say. Only when you are sure they have said all they want to say, should you then start talking. By then, of course, they will be ready to hear you and you may well have something useful to communicate.

This kind of mutual listening can only happen when I cease to be the centre of my own thoughts—in other words, when God takes the place of number one, not just as an object of worship but as a constant factor in everyday life. And this listening business is not to be limited to serious, deep conversations and counselling sessions. It applies to the everyday chatty conversations we have at bus stops and supermarkets.

When next you ask someone, 'How are you?', decide to *mean* it and really listen to the answer. It might take a long time, of course, but you might do a great deal of encouraging as a result.

---

Is the idea of listening new to you?
If not, how are you progressing as a listener?
If so, is there anything you should do about it?

---

# 10
# Anchor person

I like to think that Barnabas was like Terry Waite. Terry Waite had a worldwide reputation for diplomacy, patience and courage as the Archbishop of Canterbury's special envoy, concerned especially for the release of hostages. As a hostage himself he suffered nearly five years of solitary confinement in the Lebanon and amazed the watching world by the lucid and energetic speeches he made at the time of his release in 1991.

Terry is a huge, bearded, smiling man, well over six feet tall and by no means thin. He radiates compassion and encouragement, though he can be a tough negotiator. He had said, when asked about the secret of his success as a diplomat, that his chief weapon was listening to the views and feelings of the protagonists—trying to understand where they stood. And he had been ready to fly anywhere at any time to secure the release of a hostage. He did not always succeed, and his ministry, for such it surely was, was always under threat. But how similar to Barnabas! — a man ready to be posted here and there in the Lord's service.

# Shuttle diplomacy

Since he had already travelled from his native Cyprus to Jerusalem to join the church there, Barnabas was familiar with the open road and the open sea. We have already mentioned some of his journeys. The travelogue is quite breath-taking.

When the church in Antioch began to welcome Gentiles (non-Jews) as members, news reached the ears of the church at Jerusalem 'and they sent Barnabas to Antioch' (Acts 11:22).

Very soon, he saw the need for reinforcements so 'Barnabas went to Tarsus to look for Saul' (verse 25).

The Antioch Christians sent their Christian aid to Jerusalem 'by Barnabas and Saul' (verse 30).

'When Barnabas and Saul had finished their mission, they returned from Jerusalem...' (12:25).

Almost immediately, it seems, 'the Holy Spirit said, "Set apart for me Barnabas and Saul for the work to which I have called them", and off they went on the first missionary journey to Cyprus, Barnabas' home, and then to the South of Asia Minor, Perga, Iconium, Antioch-in-Pisidia, Derbe, Lystra, Attalia and back to Antioch-in-Syria, where they had started from (Acts 14). They stayed there 'a long time' (verse 28).

When a dispute arose concerning Christians receiving the Jewish rite of circumcision, the Antioch church sent two representatives to the Council of Jerusalem (Acts 15). Paul and Barnabas of course. When the Council had decided what to do it sent Paul and Barnabas back to Antioch with their decisions. In case it should be thought that these journeys were easy, note a phrase in the letter of commendation: 'Barnabas and Paul— men who have risked their lives for the name of our Lord Jesus Christ' (verse 26).

After another period at Antioch (verse 35) and the quarrel, Barnabas and Mark were off to Cyprus again (verse 39).

Is this becoming tedious and repetitive? Luke perhaps thought so because Barnabas disappears from the narrative at this point and the rest of Acts is focused on Paul. But enough has been seen of him to describe a man of great energy and uncomplaining willingness to be sent on errands hundreds of miles for the benefit of the churches. It looks very likely that he made many more trips, not recorded in Acts. He was *available* and he was *reliable*—two very important characteristics for the encourager.

Barnabas was the sort of man you could look up to. He may not have been as tall as Terry Waite, but he was assumed to be the king of the gods even in the presence of Paul, as we saw in the last chapter, and he became known, not merely as a disciple or learner/follower of Jesus, but as an apostle. At least, Paul seems to bracket him with himself and the other apostles in 1 Corinthians 9:6. An apostle was one who had seen the Lord and had a direct commission from him. We don't know how Barnabas qualified for this mention by Paul but we do know that he fulfilled the same functions and was regarded with esteem as a builder of people.

It has been said that our Christian duty is to find out what God is doing and then go and do it with him. Loyalty and availability, reliability in God's service are the qualities of encouragement which build up other people. Barnabas incorporated all those characteristics.

# 'Hypocrites as well'

Neighbours of old Mr and Mrs Staindrop were astonished to hear screams of laughter coming from their flat. In fact they were astonished to hear any sound at all coming from their flat. The Staindrops were very quiet. They 'kept themselves to themselves'; good neighbours in the sense that they were no trouble to anybody, but not given to company, let alone parties. Mrs Staindrop was confined to her chair anyway and Bert patiently took her to the shops once a week, to the church once a week (though he didn't stay) and to the post office for the pension once a week. No-one knew why she had to come with him to the post office, but it was a sign of her independence to be present when the money was handed over.

The Staindrops had had no children and therefore no grandchildren came to disturb the even tenor (boring repetition, some people thought) of their ways. Young people were aliens from another planet. Frequently Bert would read an item from the newspaper or see a news bulletin on T.V. which confirmed his view that the young nowadays are totally irresponsible. He would sometimes leave the set tuned to 'Top of the Pops' for a few minutes to demonstrate what he always said, that the young were noisy, degenerate and feckless. All had been well until the sixties. It was the Beatles and Cliff Richards who were to blame. He always added an 's' to annoy his wife, who responded, '*Richard*, dear, but he's a Christian, you know.' This only gave Bert a chance to expand on his theme that young people were rotten through and through, and if they pretended to be Christian that only added hypocrisy to their failings *and* if Cliff was nearly 50 and no longer young then he ought to have discovered the error of his ways by now.

So when Gavin Morrison arrived one Saturday morning in November, following the Vicar's request, his reception was somewhat cool. Bert was prepared to believe that he was as bad as the Beatles, probably a thief, certainly a hypocrite and a pi 'do-gooder'. His wife had gently reminded him that Gavin had been the only person who had brought her a cup of coffee after church, which brought the response, 'I thought all the others were supposed to be Christians. If there's only one who can bother to bring you coffee, then they're *all* a load of hypocrites', and she wished she hadn't mentioned it.

'There's one good thing anyway,' said Bert, on the morning Gavin was due to arrive. 'He won't last long. They never do. The Christian ones are worse than the others. He'll be off to a prayer meeting next time, or a pilgrimage to Mecca or somewhere.'

'Mecca's for Moslems, dear,' said Mrs Staindrop patiently.

'Well, how am I supposed to know that? He'll be going there

wherever it is.' Bert put his pipe firmly back into his mouth and his paper firmly back in front of his face.

So it had been something of a surprise to find that Gavin Morrison was not only quiet, polite and hard working, but that he had shortish hair, did not appear to be on drugs and returned regularly once a month throughout the winter. As Bert got to know Gavin he thawed a little and even suggested that he would value a few things brought from the shops every now and then (and for Bert to be willing to ask for help from anyone was a mark of recognition).

Now Gavin was not remarkably good at gardening. Especially as spring was followed by summer and the small Staindrop backyard threatened to grow itself into the house, Gavin was put through his paces by Bert, who watched him like a hawk and directed which plants were to be adjudged weeds and which were the blooms which had only missed the Chelsea Flower Show by inches. And all the time Gavin's mind was on the 'A' level homework he would have to do in the afternoon instead of concentrating on the fortunes of Wimbledon Football Club. No. Gavin was not gifted, either with green fingers or with a way with old people, but he was a determined and reliable young man and he hated to let anybody down.

This was the quality which delighted Mrs Staindrop and even gradually melted Bert into grudgingly admitting that 'Gavin isn't as bad as most of them'. And this was why the Staindrops had taken the unheard of step of inviting Gavin to tea with a few of his friends.

Five young people, boys and girls, all crowding into the Staindrops! No wonder the neighbours talked! And Gavin showed them a side of his personality that they hadn't met before. He could laugh and tell jokes and entertain them. It was altogether a very happy occasion and it resulted in two of the girls offering to do the Staindrop shopping on a regular weekly basis. Bert couldn't understand it. *They* didn't seem to be on drugs either. And they kept coming, week after week, and arranged for someone else to come when they went on holiday.

No great gifts. Just willingness to help and to go on helping.

When someone reliable is needed to do some regular task, are you able to offer? And do you keep it up?

# 11
# My goodness?

**W**hen Barnabas came to Antioch and saw what was happening, he encouraged the Christians. And he was described in Acts 11:24 as 'a good man, full of the Holy Spirit and faith'. A good man. Gavin Morrison was good. In fact at school his goodness was the cause of much mirth. He was known as 'Gavin the Good', not as a title of honour, but as a taunt. They fell about with laughter. He was a 'do-gooder', they said. He made them sick. Goody-goody.

Goodness does not get a positive rating nowadays. We tend to be shy of it as a word. Yet it is one of the fruits of the Spirit: 'Love, joy, peace, patience, kindness, goodness...' (Galatians 5:22). Goodness. It sounds bland and unexciting. A whole chapter on goodness? What a challenge! Who will press on to read it to the end? Yawn, yawn.

What has gone wrong? Unless they were all totally insincere, our Victorian ancestors really valued goodness. Deeds of kindness and charity and courageous rescues of maidens in distress were the stuff of the popular novel. Today the whole thing has turned sick. The hero who rescues the maiden in distress will be seen to have failed to fulfil himself if he doesn't get her to bed in the process. Values have been turned upside down in the popular mind, or at least in the popular press and television drama. Other and more erudite books have examined the reasons for this reversal of values—the philosophical change which filters down to the popular drama, the effects of two world wars, secularism, the shift from duties to rights, from community to self and so much more... And one of the chief victims is goodness.

# Negative and positive goodness

Christians too avert their eyes from goodness. It sounds so weak, negative and abstract. The image of little Lord Fauntleroy floats through the open window of a summer's evening with the young George Washington who never told a lie. We use images to describe the pale do-gooder: 'butter wouldn't melt in his mouth', we say, 'he couldn't hurt a fly'. A huge entertainment industry has delighted the western world for the past twenty and more years based on Charlie Brown, the archetypal well meaning, wishy-washy good person who never succeeds at anything. We begin to believe that goodness is synonymous with failure. 'Be good, sweet maid, and let who will be clever.' Even the Victorians saw it coming.

And we swallow this. We come to believe it. We accept a negative definition of goodness, an agenda provided for us by the world in general and we fail to put in its place the idea of a healthy, positive goodness which the word originally conveyed.

The Greek word used in the New Testament is *agathos*, which seems to have meant basically 'admirable'. That is, not so much a correct way of behaving but a style of living which will excite general admiration. That is the feel of the original word.

The English word 'good' today is defined by the Concise Oxford Dictionary as 'having the right qualities, satisfactory, adequate; *a good fire* (not too small or dull): *good health*, freedom from illness'. Thus far has the word become insipid and negative.

Barnabas was a good man, 'full of the Holy Spirit and faith'. Wide areas of the Christian church today emphasize being filled with the Holy Spirit, a very positive, powerful, literally dynamic activity. Others may concentrate more on the power of a living faith, the mountains that may be removed by faith, the prayer of faith... But is there a noticeable section of the church which thrives on 'goodness'? I haven't met it. Goodness has lost its power to stimulate the imagination—its cutting edge has been blunted. It has become a negative and *dis*couraging concept.

Now this is where encouragement comes in, because it is very close to the idea of goodness. The good person (Barnabas) is the encourager. Not merely the person who does *not* do certain bad things ('thou shalt not'), but one who *does* do a lot of good things. After all, goodness is one of the characteristics of God himself (Jesus said, 'No-one is good—except God alone', Luke 18:19). Being filled with the Holy Spirit and with faith and being a great encourager were all bound up in Barnabas with goodness. That's the kind of thing we are talking about. Soundness, like the deep-toned ring of a piece of healthy timber when it is struck, contagious encouragement and bright-eyed, optimistic hope. If these things are out of fashion, then pray that they will enjoy a revival, and while we are waiting for it, let's get on and spread them!

# 'Its legs fell off'

Leaving aside for the moment the moral side of goodness, and obviously there is much to be said about what is and is not good, and concentrating on the encouragement aspect, where can we look for a renewal of this optimistic, encouraging goodness?

Basically, of course, from God. Good is what God is like (Luke 18:19). Goodness is one of the fruits of the Spirit (Galatians 5:22) and *encouragement* is one of the gifts of the Spirit we hear so much about today:

> *We have different gifts, according to the grace given us. If a man's gift is prophesying, let him use it in proportion to his faith...if it is encouraging, let him encourage.*
>
> (Romans 12:6,8)

Not all will have this special gift, but there is no doubt where it comes from. It cannot be acquired by a technique, it is a gift from God, to be prayed for, longed for and learnt.

Optimism is an aspect of good encouragement, and to some extent this is a personal or even a national characteristic. In Britain it is in short supply. American readers may know otherwise, but it appears that it flourishes on their side of the Atlantic.

Participants in the panel debate 'Any Questions' on BBC radio were asked what country they would retire to if they were obliged to leave Britain. One panellist chose the USA, on the grounds that people there were generally positive and encouraging. She said something like this:

If you have an idea or propose a scheme in Britain you will be met with a barrage of discouragement. 'Oh yes, we tried that and it didn't work'; 'Have you thought how much it will *cost*?'; 'We had one and its legs fell off'; 'Not in this country surely, no-one would support *that*'.

In America, however, according to the speaker, one's suggestions, however ill-conceived, will be met with a chorus of, 'Great idea! We're with you'; 'When do we start?'; 'How can I help?' And if the scheme turns out to be a failure, no recriminations, no 'I told you so', but 'Let's gather round and support you. What can we do?'

Whether sociologists have confirmed this national trait I do not know, but if Americans have that capacity, and I think they have, then they deserve the credit. It is *good*, it is admirable and sound. It is encouraging.

But if you don't have the gift of the Spirit to encourage people and if you're not an American, what then? We shall look at this in more detail in chapter 19. It is possible to be a little *more* optimistic than we already are, a little *more* positive and encouraging.

## Positive comeback

We have already met Timothy Monteith after a typical Sunday service in chapter 2. On that occasion nobody spoke to him at all about his sermon. The following week four people came to him after the service, one at a time.

Gina Holwell said, 'I know you want to be sure we're all listening to you. Your quote from Hebrews 3:2 was really Hebrews 3:1.'

Gordon Barber said, 'Tim, in your sermon you mentioned various overseas aid organizations, but you missed out Christian Aid. I should have thought it was better to recommend than Oxfam, for a church congregation. Not everyone likes TEAR Fund.'

Cyril Kent said, 'I wish I knew how you can use that modern Bible of yours without being ashamed of yourself!'

Jane Goodrich said, 'I can't stop, mother will be getting anxious. The sermon was rather long today.'

Fourteen people had meant to thank Timothy for his sermon but had seen others talking to him/thought he didn't know them well enough/didn't want to make him proud of himself-/just didn't bother.

A hundred and three people found the sermon helpful but had no thought at all of mentioning it.

So Timothy assumed that his sermon was a failure and went home for lunch very discouraged.

Now preachers do not want flattery, nor the kind of general comment, 'your sermon was wonderful', but it does help to have some positive comeback. Thoughtful criticism is good too. But it needs to be delivered tactfully. When a preacher asks for comment people often hurt him with their bluntness on the grounds, 'Well, he asked for it, didn't he?' But a point lovingly made will be accepted much more readily than a threatening criticism. So what might Gina, Gordon, Cyril and Jane have said?

Gina: 'I was particularly helped by your comment about X in that sermon. Oh, and just to prove that I was awake, for Hebrews 3:2 read 3:1. Or was that a deliberate mistake to see if I was?'

Gordon: 'Thank you for that mention of Y. It really was appropriate. It's something I've wondered about for some time. On the subject of organizations, I suppose you could also have mentioned Christian Aid. Did you leave it out on purpose for some reason?'

Cyril: 'That was a most helpful sermon, Timothy. The Lord spoke to me through it. I still can't cope with your modern versions of the Bible, but you're doing a good job.'

Jane should have said nothing at all if she was in a hurry!

Those responses are positive and spring from a good heart.

It has been suggested that if you want to tell a person that he's doing something badly it is best to go to him three times. First time, say, 'I do appreciate what you do'. Second time, say, 'What you are doing is well done, you know'. Third time, say, 'You do that so well, may I suggest how you might do it even better?'

If we are to encourage people we have to look (hard sometimes) for the good in them, seize on it and mention it. We have to be good people ourselves, or our encouragement will not be valued. If goodness is one of our aims then bringing hope, optimistic encouragement, to others will be one of the results.

---

Check on goodness.
Can you see it as a positive quality to get excited about?
If so, what will you do about it?
If not, what will take its place?

# 12

# The man from the ministry

**A** mission turns into a movement, a movement into a machine, and a machine into a monument. So runs the formula, over-simplified no doubt, but containing a grain or two of truth. The progression can be observed in charities, even business firms, but particularly in churches and religious movements, not least Christian ones.

The pattern is that of a few dedicated, fired-up people who are inspired with missionary fervour to spread the good news of their new-found faith. Soon others join them and some organization becomes necessary. A constitution is drawn up. Definitions are written, placing barriers between those who are 'in', the members, and those who are not yet in (or 'out'), the non-members. The movement acquires a style, a way of doing things, which endears itself to members who will one day tell their grandchildren about the grand old pioneering days. Along with basic and admirable principles are enshrined customs and habits which are not necessarily so vital but which begin to be seen as essential hallmarks of the movement, never to be abandoned. The much-publicized image of the Women's Institute as 'Jam and Jerusalem' is a good example.

As time passes and the movement's first generation passes on to the second and even third, rules harden, customs freeze, the old visions may fade and the whole thing begins to lumber forward as an end in itself, having forgotten the reasons for its own existence. It has become a machine, pounding up and down, absorbing time, energy, fuel and people, but accomplishing nothing. It is not long before this state of affairs is recognized, even by the die-hard members, and the machine is laid to rest and becomes a monument—one more good idea which ran its course and is now defunct.

This can happen to churches; in fact it has happened to churches, and is a constant danger to all Christian organizations.

In order to maintain the high standards of the founding fathers, the central committee, or whatever runs the organization, lays down principles and codes of practice to be observed by all members, nationwide or worldwide. This is clearly necessary. Splinter groups with weird ideas can easily spring from the original stock. A good ideal is worth preserving.

The problem arises when the central committee loses its flexibility, imagination and sense of humour. Committees are not the first port of call when one is looking for flexibility, imagination and humour anyway. An inquisitorial cloud tends to descend on the whole organization. Witch hunts are organized to root out those who step out of line. Again, some kind of control may well be necessary. Notorious evil doing is too much condoned in our churches. We need a good dose of Paul-to-the-Corinthians, telling us to behave ourselves, but it can so easily sink to rivalry, point-scoring and church power-politics, nit-picking and negativity.

I am appalled at the kind of feuds which so often appear in the Christian press under the guise of book reviews. On the one hand, the condescending, sometimes sneering review that says, 'This is not a book that appeals to me, but it is just the sort of book which people who like such books will enjoy.'

On the other hand we have the journal which is much more concerned to advise its readers to avoid taint or blemish than to assess a book positively. Grudgingly it may admit, 'There is much that is good here, but on page 195 the author's real view on the millennium can be surmised because he fails to mention x. This means of course that the whole book is suspect and should be read with great caution and not given to the young people.' That kind of journal will be unlikely to review *this* book in those terms—it will ignore it altogether.

We are back again to slinging mud and losing ground. Healthy criticism and positive approval go together to encourage and build up. But there is a negative spirit abroad which delights to pull down, to find points to disagree with. Of course we must protest loudly if the truth is misrepresented, but I am talking about matters of detail, ways in which things are done and said which are not wrong but different from what the reviewer likes. The mission is already a movement and is well on the way to becoming a machine when this kind of in-fighting takes place, and what a tragedy that it happens under the sign of the cross, that great symbol of reconciliation.

God in heaven must surely weep, as Jesus did over Jerusalem, when he sees his children tearing each other apart in this very childish manner, and Satan must rub his hands in glee as he sees the Enemy's servants turning their energies in on each other instead of uniting to take the essentials of their gospel to the world.

# Gentiles are people too

The church in Jerusalem was both a mission and a movement when the news came from Antioch of a great turning to Christ. It was, as J. B. Phillips has called it, 'the young church in action'. It had had no time yet to allow its ways of doing things to harden into prejudices. Its days of power and glorious evangelism were still fresh—many were being saved daily, the sick were being healed, the poor heard the good news and the church was spreading, whether by mission or by dispersion caused by persecution, throughout the known world. There seemed to be nothing that the young church could not accomplish. It would, by the power of God, turn the whole world upside down...

But.

Must there always be a 'but'? It seems so. This young church consisted entirely of Jews. Of course it did. The Jews were God's chosen people. The Old Testament was their Scripture. God was their God. Admittedly he had made the world and the whole universe but he had revealed himself to the Jews, his people. And Jesus was a Jew, the greatest of all Jews, the Messiah, sent as he himself had said, to the lost sheep of the house of Israel.

Non-Jews, Gentiles, were people too, some of them very nice people. They even endowed synagogues and said complimentary things about the Temple. Well they would, when they recognized a good thing, wouldn't they? But now the unthinkable was happening. Gentiles were claiming to be Christians! It wasn't just that Jews were prejudiced against them. The very possibility of their being able to participate in God's plan of salvation hadn't occurred to the Jewish Christians at all.

But Peter the apostle had had an extraordinary experience, a vision on the housetop just before lunch one day. ('Well,' said some, 'he was obviously hungry and the sun was too hot. You should never have visions on an empty stomach.') A sheet had been let down from heaven containing all sorts of forbidden meat, still on four legs, and a voice had told him to 'get up, kill and eat'. Three times Peter had said, 'No Lord, I can't obey you, it's against my religion', but God had not accepted his scruples and had sent him to a centurion, Cornelius, who had asked to become a Christian. Peter couldn't maintain his religion in the face of this kind of power-persuasion from God's Holy Spirit so he preached the good news and many Gentiles became believers and the Spirit fell on them too.

Well, perhaps this kind of aberration could be contained in a corner. There was no need for everyone to know about it. Despite the newness of the gospel and the freshness of their faith the Jerusalem church had inherited, from their ancestors reaching back for millennia, the idea that God was *their* God and that the Gentiles were inferior beings. The church's beliefs in all the essentials of the faith were impeccable, but it was blind at this point. And it could hardly be otherwise. Try explaining to a fish that people can swim too...

But worse was to come. News reached the church in Jerusalem that the mission at Antioch was succeeding beyond their hopes and many were coming to faith there. But, horror of horrors, Gentiles again! Antioch was a large and cosmopolitan place and the new church there opened its doors to anyone who believed that Jesus had died for their sins and who showed evidence of the work of the Holy Spirit. And if God was choosing Gentiles, why shouldn't they co-operate?

The Jerusalem Committee was called, the evidence was discussed and plans were laid. These sort of goings on were 'not quite what we want', 'a dangerous precedent', 'an unfortunate example', 'will encourage the wrong kind of people to get involved', 'the right thing for the wrong reasons', 'doubtful', 'a local initiative that does not have the backing of the committee'. It's easy to make fun of them, but most of us would have taken the same line, given their background and the facts as they had them. The problem was, 'What shall we do?' And the obvious answer was, 'Send Barnabas up there to solve the problem. Send the special envoy, the negotiator, the diplomat. He'll sort them out if anybody can. Yes, that's right. Send Barnabas. Some of these preachers-to-the-Gentiles come from Cyprus. Perhaps they'll listen to Barnabas.'

## 'He was glad'

So off went Barnabas. We have already seen Acts chapter 11 from a number of points of view, but now let's see the whole picture. Barnabas arrived (verse 23) probably not knowing what to expect. He had no doubt heard of Peter's experience with

Cornelius and was armed with the Jerusalem church's authority to judge and to warn, even to discipline. So what did he see when he arrived?

He saw the evidence of the grace of God. A 'great number of people' had 'believed and turned to the Lord' (verse 21). What better evidence of God's grace could there be? Here they were rejoicing that Jews *and* Gentiles could be saved together. What Barnabas did about it reveals the man at his best:

> He was glad and encouraged them all to remain
> true to the Lord with all their hearts. He was a
> good man, full of the Holy Spirit and faith, and
> a great number of people were brought to the
> Lord.
>
> (verses 23-24)

Yet more people brought to the Lord. And why? Because, in his gladness, Barnabas *encouraged* them. His was not the temper of the father who says, 'Go and find out what young Tim is doing and tell him to stop it.' No, he saw the evidence first, before judging. He had not come determined in advance that he would suffocate this activity. He saw the evidence, made up his mind and encouraged them. And the result was yet more believers.

Yet he could so easily have observed coldly, taken these evangelists aside and warned them not to go on in this way—that their energies were best reserved for the Jews, God's elect. The growth of the church could well have been stopped by such 'correct' but ill-judged advice.

Instead he chose to throw in his hand with the work that God was doing and has gone down in history as a glad and good man.

---

Which groups or individuals do you find yourself criticizing? How can you best encourage them instead?

---

# 13
# Paroxysm

**H**ave you noticed how often Christian paperbacks give you only the positive side of life? The stories all have happy endings, the missionaries tell you how the church is growing, the books on prayer tell you of wonderful answers, the books on healing contain lots of miracles...

But surely, we protest, life isn't like that! So often it's ordinary and boring and miracles don't happen and God seems a million miles away. As soon as we've said that we feel guilty because these people are telling us how it is for them and we are saying, in effect, it's not like that for me and it's not likely to be either. And of course it isn't! And we feel indignant as well.

So are we going to hear only success stories, whether they

be from Canwell Park or Antioch? No, because our source, for Barnabas anyway, is the Bible, and the Bible is never triumphalist. It tells it as it is. It has no heroes. If Thomas doubted his master, it tells us so. If Peter denied his Lord, the record is unsparing in its detailed description. Even Barnabas was not perfect.

# Lightness of heart

Jane Goodrich was encouraged. She still hadn't broken her silence with Gina, but she had felt so much better after her long talk with Timothy and Diana. They had agreed that she didn't need to retire from the church council, but much more importantly, they had all spoken frankly and had exchanged honest opinions about each other in a very open way and had felt much closer to one another as a result:

Jane was one of those people who feels that everything goes wrong for them. Some people call them martyrs. Others say rather unkindly that they enjoy martyrdom. But Jane had always been surrounded by her mother. That was what it felt like. Sometimes she indulged in day-dreaming, wondering what freedom would be like when her mother finally—but no! The thought was sinful. How could she ever think of such a thing? Her mother was *her* mother and she, Jane Goodrich, had to carry her and she could never put her down.

That was the ever-present background to Jane's life. But she also had an unhappy knack of attracting disasters, small or great. Did she not always seem to upset Vivien James when she tried to encourage her? Was it not her own fault that the Gina Holwell/Gordon Barber fiction had been spread? Was it not her own wrong reaction that had caused all that trouble with the Vicar over the church council? This was no new thing. Jane had become used to believing that if anything was going to go wrong then it would happen to her, or be her fault.

She was particularly pleased, therefore, that Timothy had taken so much time with her and listened to her—not just to her problems but to *her*. Perhaps the direction of her life was changing at long last. There was no blinding light or great revelation but it was encouraging. So she wondered how best to express this new found lightness of heart. Whom could she help? Why, Vivien James of course! Who else? Diana had promised to come and sit with mother tomorrow evening. An ideal time to call on Vivien. So Jane spent more time than usual praying about how she could really get across to Vivien that she ought to be strong and snap out of her shyness. She would stop pushing and just go and *encourage* her.

# Flashpoint

Vivien had had a particularly difficult day at school and was now faced with a heap of ironing (why is it always *ironing*?), several lessons to get organized for tomorrow and three urgent telephone calls that could not be postponed. Imagine her annoyance therefore when she had just got her books arranged on the table and was about to begin her preparation, when a ring at the doorbell wrenched her mind back to the fact that this evening was pressured. Who *ever* could that be? Double-glazing, cavity-wall installation, JWs, police to tell me that Walter's had an accident...all these possibilities ran through her racing mind between the sitting room and the front door. And there stood—Jane.

*Oh no! Not Jane Goodrich! I really cannot cope!*

'Jane! How lovely to see you! Do come in...No, I'm not too busy, of course not. Come and sit down.'

*I'll have to offer her coffee. And then she'll stay for hours. Oh well, perhaps if I can give her forty minutes she'll realize that I'm busy and then I can catch up later with the work.*

'It is good of you to call. How's your mother? I'll leave the kitchen door open and we can talk while the kettle boils. Do you like it white? With sugar? No, not many people do today, do they...?'

*This is awful. I just feel so annoyed. Lord, please give me patience and help me not to say something I shouldn't.*

Jane was speaking. Vivien wasn't really listening. Her mind had gone into overdrive and it felt as if she was losing her control of the helter-skelter of resentment that was revolving more and more rapidly. What was Jane talking about?

*Not that again! Not me needing to pull myself together!*

No, actually Jane wasn't saying that at all.

'Perhaps it hasn't happened to me often enough,' she was saying, 'but I've found things so encouraging over the past few days that I felt I wanted to share a little joy with someone. Do you ever get that feeling? I expect you probably do, but I don't. And I thought, "Vivien". How often have I said the wrong things to Vivien! I know she's shy and withdrawn and she doesn't believe in herself and I've tried to tell her so and how she needs to pull herself together. Well, I'll go and apologize. I'll go and tell her that I've been wrong to do that. What Vivien needs is not advice, but encouragement. I've found that to be true myself. I'll go and do things differently this time. I'll go and have a nice chat with her—spend some time just being cosy together. It's so soothing and friendly...'

'SHUT UP!'

'I beg your pardon, dear?'

'I said, "SHUT UP!" I can't take any more! I've got far too much to do, and I can't...' Vivien burst into a flood of tears.

'But Vivien, you said...'

'I know what I said, but, but, please go away. Don't say anything else. Just go away.'

Jane went away.

Two hours later, Walter returned to find his wife ironing.

'Hello Viv, everything OK?'

'Yes, thanks.'

'No problems?'

'One, but I think it's improving.'

'What happened, then?'

'Jane Goodrich came round to tell me to snap out of it. And I did.'

# Saint Paul and Saint Barnabas

We encountered the difference of opinion between Barnabas and Paul in chapter seven. Let's look a little more closely at what happened. The brief account in Acts 15:36-41 tells us all that we need to know, but the imagination may reconstruct the scene.

Paul and Barnabas had been back for some time from their missionary foray into Cyprus and Asia Minor. They were kept busy teaching the Antioch church and no doubt seeing a lot of new life developing there. But Paul had left part of himself in the young churches of Asia Minor. He felt an increasing desire to go back and visit them and encourage them. Some might have gone off the rails already, others might have collapsed completely. Some might be flourishing. News leaked through every now and then, but nothing very clear.

If Paul was thinking strategically, so was Barnabas. He had a great concern to promote and train new workers. If they were to go back on that long haul around Lystra and Derbe and all those difficult places, at least it would be good to give some in-service training to a younger man. John Mark was Barnabas' cousin (Colossians 4:10). The conversation probably went something like this:

'I think you're right, Paul. We shouldn't put too much into one church—the others need help too. But don't you think we ought to take someone with us who can learn the job? A younger man perhaps?'

'Yes, you're right. Do you have anyone in mind?'

'John Mark.'

'*John Mark*! Of all the names you might have mentioned, that's about the least likely to ring bells with me.'

'Yes, but he's a good man. He needs someone to trust him. Give him some responsibility and he'll blossom.'

'We gave him some responsiblity the first time and as soon as we reached the mainland he was off home like a scalded cat. He's not the kind of person we need for this tough work, Barnabas, and you know it!'

'How can anyone ever develop if you don't give them a second chance? None of us is an instant success. You've had your ups and downs yourself, you know.'

'Barnabas, your mind is getting clouded and I think I know why. You're flying in the face of the evidence. It's all because he's your cousin, isn't it? It's a family matter and you don't want to lose your family reputation.'

'Paul, that's a very nasty suggestion. I wouldn't have expected it from you. It doesn't matter whose family he belongs to. We're all in God's family now, anyway. And as for evidence, how can you assume that Mark will always be the same? "Not the kind of person we need"! Neither were you until the Lord took hold of you and changed you. With the power of the Holy Spirit Mark will be a changed man!'

'Oh, you're bringing in the Holy Spirit on your side of the argument now, are you? Well in that case, whose idea was it to take John Mark in the first place? *Yours.* Yes it was, my dear Barnabas. Yours. Was it the Holy Spirit's idea? No it was not. The Holy Spirit said, "Set apart for me Barnabas and Saul for the work to which I have called them." Those words are recorded in the minutes of the church meeting. He didn't say anything about John Mark. He came tagging along because you thought he might be of some help. So don't pretend that the Lord wanted him with us. It's bad enough your trying to advance your chicken-hearted relations, but to have the affrontery to pretend that it's the will of *God*, well that's going too far. My dear Barnabas...'

'SHUT UP!'

'I beg your pardon?'

'I said, "Shut up". *You've* gone too far. Take who you like to Perga in Pamphylia. I'm not coming with you for a start. I'll take Mark and we'll go to Cyprus. We're better off going in opposite directions!'

If those who rightly respect Saint Paul and Saint Barnabas feel that this reconstruction has become exaggerated, look closely at the word used at this point. 'They had such a sharp disagreement that they parted company' (Acts 15:39). The word translated 'sharp disagreement' is used only this once in the whole Bible. It is *paroxysmos*, 'paroxysm'. It implies an explosion of fury caused by increasing frustration. Yes, even Paul and Barnabas were human beings, capable of hurting each other, their Lord and their church. Good may well have resulted from this outburst (churches benefited in Cyprus and on the mainland and both Mark *and* Silas were trained), but the paroxysm itself was very painful.

If we were in danger of treating Barnabas as a hero who had no faults, a stray reference in Galatians (2:11-13) shows again that he was not always at his best.

The influx of Gentiles had caused problems with the Jewish core of the church. Ought Gentiles to be allowed to join fully into church membership even though they were not circumcised and did not subscribe to other Jewish customs? This kind of thing was causing a split—Jews were ready to welcome Gentiles as Christians but their disgusting habits and lack of holiness (in Jewish eyes) made them unacceptable as brothers and sisters. Peter tried to compromise. He had full fellowship with Gentiles wherever he went, but when an official party from the Jerusalem church came to see them he withdrew from them and started acting as a strict Jew again. This compromise was hypocrisy in Paul's eyes, and he said so in no uncertain terms: 'The other Jews joined him in his hypocrisy, so that by their hypocrisy even Barnabas was led astray' (Galatians 2:13).

# Real world

Led astray, lost his temper. Barnabas seems to have had feet of clay. Jane Goodrich and Vivien James had their paroxysm on a different subject but didn't appear to be behaving as Christians should do. Wouldn't it be better to hide all these discouraging goings on in a book on encouragement?

No, for three reasons.

First, because it is wrong to hide the truth. The Bible doesn't, so why should any lesser book? An encourager will get discouraged. Good intentions will backfire. This is a real world. We cannot yet escape from it.

Second because, even if we do have feet of clay, God knows about that and he knows that we all do. What matters is not what our feet are made of but where we are standing. On sand or on the Rock?

Third, because if great encouragers fall down sometimes it may be an encouragement to us, lesser encouragers as we are, to know that we share problems. Barnabas didn't lose his title

'Son of encouragement' because he argued with Paul. Paul didn't forfeit his apostleship because he was rude to Barnabas. Then in this unpleasant area we can find some hope. There is such a thing as forgiveness...

---

Have you met examples of 'paroxysms' recently?
What have you done about them? How can you use them in an encouraging way?

# 14

# Satan the discourager

Once upon a future time, Satan, sensing that his days were numbered and the day of reckoning approaching, decided to cut his losses and make a last dishonest profit by selling his tools. So he advertised the sale and laid out all the tools of his trade, the instruments with which he had tempted and troubled mankind over thousands of years.

Set aside on a table by itself was one very unpleasant looking instrument, very well-worn and obviously much used. And the asking price was out of all proportion to those of the other tools (and the prices were all extortionate!). When asked why that instrument was worth so much more than all the others Satan replied, 'That one is called Discouragement, and that has been my best and most effective weapon.'

Throughout the history of mankind Satan has been the Discourager, the avowed opponent of the Creator who, in his love, desires to build up. Satan desires to tear down. He appears first in the guise of the serpent in Genesis 3, tempting Adam and Eve to disbelieve and disobey God. 'Did God really say, "You must not eat...?" ' He is the one who hints and casts doubt. 'God wouldn't do a thing like that. Surely not.' Throughout the Bible, until he is thrown finally into the lake of fire in the book of Revelation, Satan is always the liar, the whisperer, the devourer.

'Your enemy the devil', writes Peter, 'prowls around like a roaring lion looking for someone to devour. Resist him...' (1 Peter 5:8-9).

God wants to make, Satan to destroy; God to grow people, Satan to consume people.

# Frustration

In our snapshots of the church in Canwell Park we have already seen numerous examples of Satan at work. Who but he could have arranged it that people all intending to help each other, and with the best of motives, should end up by destroying each other?

Who managed for a long time to blind the minds of Cyril Kent and Bob Renshaw to the good intentions of each other? Whose but a devilish intelligence could have arranged for Mrs Goodrich to be watching just as Gordon appeared to be leaving Gina in her dressing gown? Who would have the patience, year after weary year, to make sure that Jane should labour on, getting more and more discouraged and depressed, and that so many 'coincidences' should conspire to 'happen' to her? And who but Satan could arrange that so many ministers are like Timothy, conscientious, faithful servants of their Lord, yet misunderstood, pressurized and exhausted by the very people who ought to be supporting them? And those people, good Christians too, grumbling and discouraging each other, seeing the worst in their ministers, complaining about their shortcomings. Who but Satan could have built up such a pressure in Vivien James that she exploded in the face of Jane? And who but Satan could have come between those two great disciples, Paul and Barnabas?

If Satan did not exist we should have to invent him to explain how so many things go wrong when good people try to the best of their ability to get things right. Paul himself expressed the frustration that he felt in his letter to the Romans:

> *I have the desire to do what is good, but I cannot*
> *carry it out. For what I do is not the good I want*
> *to do; no, the evil I do not want to do—this I keep*
> *on doing. Now if I do what I do not want to do,*
> *it is no longer I who do it, but it is sin living in*
> *me that does it.*
>
> (Romans 7:18-20)

He talked about 'sin' working in him, 'another law at work in the members of my body, waging war against the law of my mind and making me a prisoner' (verse 23). This was no abstract principle, this was a personal intelligence at work, undermining Paul's will to do what was right, discouraging him at every turn, to such an extent that he was obliged to cry out, 'What a wretched man I am! Who will rescue me?' (verse 24). Paul didn't need to invent Satan. He knew him and his methods at first hand. He even saw his chronic ailment, whatever it was, as 'a messenger of Satan, to torment me' (2 Corinthians 12:7).

What is happening? One of God's saints going unhealed despite repeated prayer, tormented by sin which he cannot escape? The church of God down the ages torn apart by jealousies and petty rivalry, by misunderstandings and evil coincidences? Is Satan so alive and well that God himself has abdicated? If sin is so strong that Paul could say that it was not himself but sin at work in him that was responsible for his actions, have we no free will left? Is Satan God after all? Perish the very thought, but some of these reflections begin to give us that impression.

On the other hand, is the idea of Satan one big cop-out?

Are we not blaming a person we call Satan for our own sins—refusing to take responsibility for them, like the child accused of breaking a cup, who blames the rabbit, who happens to be in its hutch at the time, and then bursts into tears of frustration because nobody will believe him? If Satan did not exist we'd have to invent him. Perhaps that's exactly what we have done.

# Evil intelligence

This question deserves some serious thought. There are many Christians who have little or no difficulty in believing in God, who find belief in a personal devil very hard. The idea of Satan seems childish, a rationalization of our own evil, which we blame on him. To those people I feel inclined to say, 'Don't worry, far be it from me to set about persuading you of the existence of Satan. Our energies are better used in persuading people of the existence of God. But you must admit that the idea of a personal, evil intelligence does justice to the facts better than any other explanation. Have you never felt tempted? Who is tempting you? You're not tempting yourself! So let's at least agree that "Satan" is shorthand for what appears to be an evil intelligence.'

But now I have a problem. Apart from my experience of temptation, which makes belief in a personal devil very probable, I also find the existence of Satan, the devil, assumed from the beginning to the end of the Bible. For some people that is conclusive. It is for me. But for some people, my saying 'never mind whether you believe in Satan or not' is tantamount to saying that I don't care too much for the authority of the Bible. Take it or leave it. I don't mean that. But people need to move forward slowly and be encouraged, not browbeaten. We shall look at the smouldering wick principle later on, but don't use the Bible as a battering ram. If it is authoritative it will establish its own authority in due course.

To those who find it more comfortable to see Satan as nothing but a helpful explanation of the facts of sin and temptation I would just mention one thing. If he were to turn out to be real after all, that's just the kind of idea he'd like you to have. He could then work away incognito without attracting unwelcome attention to himself.

(It would be ungrateful not to acknowledge C S Lewis at this point. The whole subject is treated so well in *The Screwtape Letters* that little more need be said here.)

The opposite face of this problem, however, is to see Satan under every cornflake—to attribute to Satan every disease, every exhibition of ill-temper, every failure of ours to be what we should be. Isn't that what Paul was doing in Romans chapter 7? He gave up in despair, didn't he?

No, he didn't actually. After his impassioned outburst, 'Who will rescue me from this body of death?', he answered himself at once, 'Thanks be to God—through Jesus Christ our Lord!' (Romans 7:24-25), and then went on to write that superb expression of confident faith, Romans 8, beginning, 'Therefore, there is now no condemnation for those who are in Christ Jesus'. No, God hasn't abdicated. Read the rest of Romans 8 if you are tempted(!) to think that he has. But Satan has certainly been allowed a lot more rope than we would like. We don't know why—perhaps our free will would be curtailed if he were totally bound.

At the cross, Satan was defeated and began his ever-accelerating plunge towards the bottomless pit. 'Having disarmed the powers and authorities, he (Jesus) made a public spectacle of them, triumphing over them by the cross' (Colossians 2:15). But in his fall Satan is doing as much damage as he can before he hits the bottom. Like a cat in a china cupboard as it falls from the top shelf, knocking cups and plates off all the other shelves on its way down. Not by accident, but by sinister and intelligent design, Satan is destroying whatever good he can see, while still there is time.

Remember his most effective instrument? It is with discouragement that he infects the people of God. And he will use whatever form of discouragement comes most readily to hand in his desperate struggle to damage his Enemy's purposes.

# Worry

Jane Goodrich arrived home in tears. Her mother was already calling out to her as soon as she opened the door, 'Jane! Jane! What's the matter? Come up and tell me about it!'

Diana Monteith, who was at that moment reading a particularly amusing extract from *Persuasion*, was shocked at the abruptness of this cry, cutting across her reading without warning. She put the book down and awaited developments. Jane appeared briefly at the doorway, muttered something about going to lie down and coming back to give her mother her final drink of the day, and disappeared into her bedroom, slamming the door as she did so.

The book was forgotten in a moment. Mrs Goodrich sat up erect in bed. 'Things seem to be going wrong with Jane recently,' she said ominously. 'It's not right.'

Diana remembered their very positive talk with Jane and murmured that not everything was going wrong surely. She had decided to leave Jane alone at this point and stay by her post with the old lady.

'Too many things are going wrong. I worry about her. I lie awake at night worrying about her. I'm her mother, you see.'

'Yes of course, but worrying won't help Jane. Have you tried praying for her?'

'Prayer? Oh yes, I've tried prayer. It doesn't work—and you know it deep down really, but you have to pretend it does, being the vicar's wife and all.'

'Does worry work any better?' asked Diana, really wanting to know.

'It's not a question of whether it works. I'm her mother and it's my job to worry about her. She hasn't got anybody else. I've worried about her ever since before she was born and I shall go on worrying about her until I die—or she does. And if something happens to me I don't know *what* will happen to her because there'll be no-one to worry about her at all. Nobody else cares.'

'Do you think Jane is glad that you worry about her? Is she grateful?'

'She ought to be. I've spent my whole life worrying about her. She ought to be grateful.'

Diana began to see why Jane had so many problems. All that pressure on top of her responsibilities!

'Don't you see,' said Diana gently, 'that you are putting extra pressure on her by worrying? If she knows you are worrying it makes it harder for her. If she has a problem she has one problem. If you worry about it, she has two problems.'

'Don't try to separate me from my daughter,' said Mrs Goodrich darkly. 'She's my responsibility and I'm not going to surrender it now. If you love someone you can't help worrying about them. You can't help it, so there's an end to it.'

Diana went home that night and prayed for Jane. And for her mother. What a wonderful thing a mother's love could be. And what a terrible thing it could become if it was turned in on itself and poisoned. How easily mothering turned into smothering. Why oh why does it have to happen?

And some people don't believe in Satan!

---

Do you believe in a personal devil?
Does it matter whether you do or not?
Can you advise someone who can't help worrying about people?

---

# 15
# The Divine Encourager

Too much concentration on evil and the devil is in itself discouraging. It can be most unhealthy. If in doubt, look Up. So where can we look for encouragement? To the example of Barnabas, yes indeed. But Barnabas is nothing more than an example, a character in a book, real enough in Century One but not much use to us now. Indeed his splendid example makes us feel guilty if we fail to live up to it.

No, what we need is power—power to convert the good example into real life, to make us feel encouraged and wanted, to put backbone into us. And that power is available. Not the power of muscle, nor even of determination, but the all-conquering power of divine love, the Third Person of the

Trinity himself, the Holy Spirit. If you think of Satan as merely an evil influence you may be tempted to think of the Holy Spirit as a correspondingly good influence. But if you know him you will also know that he is real, personal and the source of all encouragement.

When Jesus promised that the Spirit would come (as recorded by John in his Gospel, chapters 14, 15 and 16), he used the word *paraklētos*. It may sound familiar. Barnabas was called 'son of *paraklēsis*', you may remember, 'son of encouragement'. So is the Holy Spirit the Encourager? Indeed he is, though the word is not used in the Bible translations. We have 'Comforter' in the King James Version, 'Counsellor' in the Revised Standard Version, 'Advocate' in the Jerusalem Bible and 'Helper' in the Good News Bible (see pages 156-159 for a further list of words).

None of these quite get at the root meaning of the word which is to 'call alongside'. Perhaps J. B. Phillips gets nearest to it when he calls him, 'the One Who is coming to stand by you'. That's a wonderful concept. When we are discouraged or afraid, the worst of it is when we are *alone*, especially during a sleepless night. If we could be assured that there is One who is coming to stand by us, our problems would be sliced in half. And we *are* assured of that very thing, by our Lord himself.

# One Encourager, four hearty cheers!

It is worth spending a few minutes looking at Jesus' words about the Spirit here, because they spell encouragement in a big way and because, as we have said, this is the very root, foundation and source of the whole movement of God's encouragement to us. John records the use of the word *paraklētos* four times. He adds a different explanation each time:

*1. The Spirit of Truth who will live in us for ever (John 14:16-17)* More about the idea of truth later on, but just look at the rest of it: the Spirit of God himself appeared to live within us, not just for a trial period on approval, but for ever. I defy anyone to produce anything more encouraging than that.

## 2. The Holy Spirit will teach you all things *(John 14:26)*

He didn't mean that for the committed Christian education is no longer needed; inspiration rules OK. In fact he went on to explain what he meant '...teach you all things and will remind you of everything I have said to you'. All things concerning Jesus. He reminded the gospel writers of all that was relevant to be recorded for the world to know, and he it is who reminds us too of the example, the teaching and supremely the death and resurrection of Jesus. When the Christian is discouraged it is a fact of experience that Jesus, his Lord, may be the last person he thinks of. It is the task of the Holy Spirit to remind us of him, to turn our thoughts back to the place where alone we find peace.

## 3. He will bear witness to me *(John 15:26)*

This suggests that the Encourager will use us to point the unbelieving world to Christ because he goes on to say, 'you also must testify, for you have been with me from the beginning'. This meant the disciples who knew Jesus in his earthly life, of course, but we are their heirs and successors.

One of the best ways of encouraging someone is to entrust them with a job. It makes them feel needed and they may well grow into the responsibility that you have placed on them (if you can stand back and not keep interfering, of course). That is just what Jesus Christ did. He left his small band of followers and entrusted them with the message of life and told them to be witnesses. What a risk he was taking! Had it not been for the promised presence of the Divine Encourager it would have been too great a risk.

## 4. He will convince the world of sin, of righteousness and of judgment *(John 16:8)*

That doesn't sound too encouraging on the surface, but we are back with the oft-repeated truth that encouragement cannot be divorced from reality. If it is, it becomes 'pie in the sky when you die', or a make-believe trip to Cloud Nine, a kind of fix on a religious drug. The harsh realities of sin and judgment are not to be ignored, yet through it all shines the prospect of righteousness and the presence of the Encourager.

Three of the four references here speak of the Spirit being sent by the Father. Jesus also says that he will send the Spirit and that he goes to the Father. The mystery of the Trinity is not the subject of this book, but what Jesus is telling us here is that *God himself* is coming to stand by us, to plead for us, to be our advocate, helper, counsellor, comforter and encourager.

Words can express no more than that.

# 'They have lovely feathers'

Gordon was trying to lead a house group. He felt that he was attempting to keep up with it rather than leading it because when they kept to the point (which was not always) they seemed to disagree. The subject, ironically, was the Holy Spirit. If he's leading us into all truth, Gordon was thinking to himself, then truth must be ten or twelve different and contradictory things all at once.

They were arguing now about how the Holy Spirit comes to Christians. Mrs Beesley had no doubts about the matter:

'The Holy Spirit is given in baptism,' she was saying. 'It says so in the Prayer Book. And then, when you're confirmed by the Bishop the Spirit comes again. That's what I was taught at St James's and the Rector there was a Canon!'

Carol Jenkins, one of the three younger people in the group, gave a stifled scream:

'But if the Spirit came at baptism, why does he need to come again when you're confirmed? All this churchy stuff doesn't make sense. Christians today are only pretending. They don't have the real thing unless they're baptized in the Spirit...'

'That's right,' Rachel interrupted excitedly. 'You need to realize how empty you are and go forward at a big rally and have hands laid on you and *Pow!* you're baptized in the Spirit. Anyone can do it. You don't need a bishop!'

'Neither do you need a big rally.' Cyril Kent was leaning forward with his Bible open at Romans 8. 'And "pow" is not a word that I find in Scripture either. The Holy Spirit is the precious possession of every believer. You can't be a second-class Christian who doesn't have the Spirit or a first-class one who does. Paul the apostle writes in Romans 8:9, "Ye are not in the flesh but in the Spirit, if so be that the Spirit of God dwell in you. Now if any man have not the Spirit of Christ, he is none of his." In other words, if you don't possess the Spirit you are not a Christian at all.'

Three people began to speak at once, so Gordon raised his voice to restore order:

'I don't think we're going to agree on this if we talk until midnight. Some of you won't like this, but I'm going to suggest that who the Spirit is is more important than how he comes to us, and that the effect he has on us is more important that what we believe about confirmation...'

'Canon George said it was baptism and confirmation,' said Mrs Beesley decidedly and folded her hands on her lap.

'Let's move on, then,' said Gordon, slightly more loudly than he need have, 'and ask what the Holy Spirit does for us.'

They were a well-informed group. The answers came thick and fast.

'Gifts, like tongues, prophecy and healing.' That was Rachel.

'And administration and helps.' That was Cyril.

'What are helps?'

'Helpers, helping. The Spirit sees to it that we get assistance when we need it.'

'Except for the flower rota,' said a soft voice which was fortunately drowned by others.

'Fruit. He gives us fruit. Love, joy, peace, patience and all that. Galatians somewhere. I remember Mrs Bennet who used to teach us in Sunday School, she had us all hanging fruit on one another and we all had nine. I don't know why it was nine. I don't remember what they all were...'

'He leads us into all truth.'

'He's the Comforter.'

'The Advocate.'

'The Helper.'

116

'The paraclete...'

Gordon realized that he shouldn't have said that. Carol, Rachel and Sharon, the third member of their alliance, all burst into peals of merriment.

'My auntie had one but it died.'

'They come from South America, don't they?'

'No, Australia.'

'Well they have lovely feathers, but they make a horrible noise!'

'Calm down, calm down,' said Gordon. 'I should have known better than to try to educate you lot! But you've collected quite a lot of good answers to the question. Can you see anything which they all have in common— gifts, fruit, truth, comfort, help...?'

'Yes, they're all for our benefit, or rather for the benefit of the church, not just for our personal pleasure. They're all positive and encouraging things.'

'Exactly,' said Gordon, delighted that someone had given the answer that he wanted, and even more so because it was Margaret who had made the point. She had been so much more alive and positive recently.

'Exactly, he is the Encourager. He is called that in John's Gospel. I can't use the Greek word now, since you people find it so amusing, but what it means is One Who comes to stand by you.

'Some of us in this church have been finding that encouragement is one of the best means of helping people—standing by them. And if you want to be an encourager, as a Christian you need to have the Holy Spirit, the source of all encouragement, at your side, giving you the gift of encouragement. Nobody mentioned that one earlier, but it's there in Romans 12:8. We have different gifts, says Paul, and if your gift is to encourage then use it to the full. Well, that's my translation.

'We are much too inclined to criticize, to break down or to preach at people. If someone says he is baptized in the Spirit and he goes round criticizing other people and spreading gossip and arguing with everyone he meets, then it's not the Holy Spirit I know.

117

'This church is growing by the grace of God, and it's growing because we are learning to appreciate one another, encourage one another and share the strength of the Spirit with each other. That growth and that strength have only one source.'

There was an impressive silence.

'If no-one has anything to add I think we should use the rest of the time praying together.'

The prayer flowed freely that night.

---

Do you see the Holy Spirit, the Encourager, in this light?
Is he standing by you?
Are you using the gift of encouragement?

# 16
# The Spirit of Truth

*When he, the Spirit of truth, comes, he will guide you into all truth...he will bring glory to me by taking from what is mine and making it known to you.*

(John 16:13-14)

The three girls surrounded Gordon in a corner. There was no way he could see to escape. The meeting had finished, the coffee and biscuits were doing the rounds and Gordon was trapped.

'What's all this you've been saying about truth and glory and all that? It don't *mean* anything! It's just words, words, isn't it? Truth and glory...'

'Yeah, she's right! The Holy Spirit isn't just truth and glory, he's God who sweeps you off your feet. The *proof* of the Spirit is people speaking in tongues. You can hear that. You can't hear truth, can you?'

'Well,' said Gordon, 'you're not giving me much of a chance to tell you what I think.'

'Go on then.'

'Yeah, go on.'

'We'll give you ten minutes.'

'No more; I've got to relieve Mum's babysitter at ten o'clock.'

'Right,' said Gordon, 'truth. If it's raining and I come in and tell you that it's stopped, that's a lie. It's untruth. If I say it's still raining, that's true.'

'This is kid's stuff.'

'Shurrup. Let him go on.'

'So,' said Gordon patiently, 'if I tell you it is raining I am witnessing to the truth. I am telling you what *is*. I am using words to describe reality. Are you with me?'

'So far.'

'So the word "truth" always means what really *is*. Not what I imagine or you think, but what is real. Now God alone knows what is really real. He is the maker of it all—the source of all truth, you might say. Because God is the foundation of reality...'

'Wait a minute, you've lost me there. This is too much like a philosophy lesson.'

'Well, look at it this way. Some people today believe that everything is just what you imagine, and I imagine and everyone else imagines. There's no *real* at all, just lots of impressions, all different.'

'OK.'

'If you're a Christian you will believe that there is a Real. "In the beginning, God." So God is real. We are all real as well, but only because he made us. We can't be more real than God is. God is real. God is truth.'

'Are you saying that truth is another name for God?'

'In a way, yes. Jesus said, "I am the way, the truth and the life." I *am* the truth. Not I *tell* the truth. So the Spirit who is also God, is called the Spirit of truth, and he will lead *us* into all truth, that is lead us to Jesus, "taking from what is mine and making it known to you". So you see, it's not just philosophy. It's all shorthand for the Spirit of Jesus drawing us to himself. The God who is real wants us to know that he's real, so he comes to us and makes us see that he's real.'

'But you said "God is truth". I thought God was love.'

'Yes, he is,' said Gordon, quite encouraged. 'But you wouldn't expect God to be just one thing. Truth is what really *is*. So is love. Both of them together. And it's the Holy Spirit leading us to him who is truth and love. That's not so different from your idea of the Spirit, is it?'

'Well, it's a long way round. I'd rather just be zapped.'

'So would I. You feel a tingling sensation *all over*!'

'That's right. I know someone who said she felt like she was on fire...'

Gordon slipped out of the corner and shook his head, half sadly and half in amusement. 'However they come to it, Lord, please may your Spirit make them free.' He walked over to join Cyril who was telling Mrs Beesley about the fallacies of baptismal regeneration.

# 'Try not to think about it'

One of the forerunners of the current spate of soap operas on radio and TV was called 'Mrs Dale's Diary'. It was a BBC radio production and it happened even before the Archers. Mrs Dale's husband was a family doctor of the old-fashioned kind. He was good at dispensing medicine, but not so hot when it came to comforting the agitated or counselling the anxious. His favourite remedy was: 'Have a nice cup of tea and try not to think about the problem.'

This recipe was used for crises and disasters as well as for encouragement when things were difficult. The cup of tea probably helped in some cases, at least the occupation of boiling a kettle was positive, but the advice given was particularly useless. It was the equivalent of a pat on the head. 'Cheer up, it may never happen' is equally pointless. It's not encouragement. It's wishful thinking.

Encouragement must have some substance to make it really encouraging. And if you're going to affirm someone you need to give them reasons for them to hold on to. Before you say something that you hope will be encouraging, anticipate the immediate question, 'why?'.

'Cheer up!'

'Why?'

I can't help sympathizing with the person who wrote: 'A voice came to me out of the gloom, "Rejoice and be glad, for things could be worse". So I rejoiced and was glad, and behold, things did get worse.'

In other words, real encouragement is to do with truth and love. To do with what really *is* and with building up. Encouragement is not telling 'white lies' about someone in the hope that it will build up their confidence. They probably won't believe you anyway, and if they do they will soon discover their mistake and won't trust you in future. So don't be tempted to tell someone how good they are at doing the flowers in church when their efforts resemble a rubbish heap in October.

What can you tell them, then, to encourage them? Obviously there are various ways of appreciating someone's genuine efforts without telling lies. Tell them how glad you are that they've done it, how good it is that they got involved. This may be just what was needed to get them going. They might improve out of all recognition and you will have gained a flower arranger.

There is, however, a possibility that they will get enthusiastic but will never improve because they are colour-blind and unconscious of form or shape. Encouraging this person is to encourage embarrassment to all concerned. It may be necessary very kindly to face them with the truth that perhaps their gifts lie elsewhere.

But be prepared for the reaction. Hopeful novelists used to send their work to Charlotte Bronte. She wrote:

*They are most difficult to answer, put off, and appease without offending, for such characters are*

*excessively touchy and when affronted turn malig-*
*nant. Their books are too often deplorable.* *

So when you tell someone gently that they are not very good at what they are hoping to do, mix in some encouragement about what else they might be gifted at, because you will be causing them pain. Try to avoid affronting them. But don't be drawn into lies, 'white lies' or half-truths. Being economical is not something you can really do with truth.

# Truth and love

So all encouragement ought to contain truth and love. Put in the 'because' before they ask 'why?'. 'I think you're an asset to the group because you are always so cheerful. Your smile is contagious.' Look out for something like that to latch on to and use it to bring positive affirmation. The love comes in the way you do it—with a smile yourself, with an arm round the shoulder or a hand on the forearm, or whatever is appropriate.

The question of physical contact is a difficult one, but there is no doubt that it is encouraging. The difficulty lies in its over-use between the sexes or its thoughtless use with people who are offended by being 'pawed' as they put it.

Studies have shown that when there is even a slight contact there is an improvement in attitude. A library assistant made it her business when serving her customers 'accidentally' to touch the hand of each one, quite unobtrusively. Not many noticed that it had happened but most, when questioned, felt that they had enjoyed being served by that particular girl. On its own a touch on the arm may make you feel a bit better but it is not the whole story. But if you can use the appropriate touch as well as the words of truth and the expression of love you will be welcomed wherever you go and you will be building up the people you meet.

Shelley Barber was not always perfect of course (of that, more

* Margaret Lane: *The Bronte Story* (Fontana, 1969), p.265.

painful revelations later) but she did seem to have a gift of saying the right thing that started people off on the right path. Her picture for Gordon has been mentioned as well as her wise words about Cyril Kent and her 'phone conversation with Timothy. She was, of course, one of those little girls who loves answering the 'phone. Her mother came in from the garden one day to find her just beginning a conversation: 'Hello, Miss Goodrich. Daddy's out and Mummy's in the garden but you can talk to me... Do you like talking to me? Timothy does... Timothy is the Vicar...Yes, I call him Timothy. He's nice. I like his voice. And I like yours. You have a nice voice... I like talking to you...'

Again, nothing profound, but Jane was encouraged. It was a statement of truth with a reason given and it was totally guileless and naive. Perhaps our encouragement needs to be more childlike. If our motives were innocent and uncomplicated we should be able to say exactly what we felt and be appreciated and be a help to each other. Sadly this is not the case, but there's no reason why we shouldn't get near to it if we can.

---

Do you know people who try to encourage you with empty flattery? Does it help? Do you know people who are willing to tell you the truth? Is that better?
Can you see how you can improve your own encouragement ministry?

---

# 17
# Why?

I t is time to answer a question: a question that worries some people, though perhaps not those who have got this far in a book about encouragement. The question is this: why do we need encouragement? Can we not do without it? Isn't there a danger that we might be getting soft, wanting to be patted and pampered? I hope we have come far enough not to believe that encouragement is like that, but the question remains, why?

The answer is twofold: because the Bible is full of it, as we have seen before, and because we function much worse without it (which is the reason why the Bible is full of it).

On pages 156-159 you will find a selection of Bible words which convey the idea of encouragement. There are more. It is a rich and varied offering. Some of those words, like 'exhort' and 'strengthen', remind us that the balance is struck between the 'loving arms' affirmation type of encouragement and the Bishop Odo of Bayeux get-up-and-go type of strengthening. There is a good example of this in 2 Corinthians 4, where Paul is reflecting that we are weak and feeble and that our strength comes from God. No patting on the head here:

> *We have this treasure in jars of clay to show that this all-surpassing power is from God and not from us. We are hard pressed on every side, but not crushed; perplexed, but not in despair; persecuted, but not abandoned; struck down, but not destroyed. We always carry around in our body the death of Jesus, so that the life of Jesus may also be revealed in our body.*
>
> (2 Corinthians 4:7-10)

In other words, we are fragile and are constantly almost destroyed. Is that encouraging? Yes, because of the 'almost'. And what stands between us and disintegration is the presence of Christ in us. If he were withdrawn, if his Spirit departed, we should collapse like a perished balloon. But he doesn't depart and we don't collapse, even if we feel like it sometimes. We have embraced death to the old life and risen again to new life—that is what baptism is all about—and so our very living depends not on ourselves, or our efforts, but on him and his presence. That is the basis of all encouragement. He loves us enough to die for us. To *die* for us. To die for *us*.

You matter that much.

If you can cope with that amazing fact it is but a short step to recognize that you don't matter to the world. As the wit once said, 'It's a case of mind over matter. I don't mind and you don't matter.' Men and women spend their lives striving to establish themselves in other people's esteem. To achieve something, to matter, to leave a mark on the world, is all their desire.

The Christian doesn't need to do that. It creeps into the

best of our intentions but there's no need. We matter because we matter to God. So we can afford to admit that we are fragile pots, easily broken. We can even delight in our own weakness. As the Lord said to Paul, 'My power is made perfect in weakness' (2 Corinthians 12:9).

# How light is your burden?

So even the grin-and-bear-it approach which Paul seems to offer contains some gems of encouragement. In other places the Bible is more obviously gentle. In the book of Numbers we read about God's everlasting arms, ready to embrace us. Psalm 23 reminds us of the shepherd, leading his people to pasture. One of the most heart-warming passages, and perhaps best known, occurs in Matthew 11:28-30:

> *Come to me, all you who are weary and burdened, and I will give you rest. Take my yoke upon you and learn from me, for I am gentle and humble in heart, and you will find rest for your souls. For my yoke is easy and my burden is light.*

There are two burdens mentioned here. The burden which the Lord gives us to carry is light. It is implied that our own burden, mentioned at the beginning, is heavy. We are wearied with it. We carry it about and find nowhere to lay it down. Nowhere, that is, until we come to Jesus and leave it thankfully at his feet. The burden he gives us to carry is by comparison, light. Why? Because if we are yoked with him, like two beasts of burden under one yoke-frame, he is sharing the load with us.

He is described here as gentle and humble of heart. Our God himself is humble! Indeed, for he came down to earth from heaven itself, to a poor stable, a vagrant life and a stark gibbet. But this humble God wants us to come to him; anyone, that is, who is weary, and aren't we all?

I am emphasizing this point because the essence of encouragement is to know that we matter. Paul expressed that in the vessels of clay picture. Our Lord expresses it in his invitation to come and be yoked to him. Come to me, come with me. Take a rest and be encouraged.

Another motive for encouragement is given by Paul in Romans 1:11-12. 'I long to see you', he says to the Roman Christians, 'so that I may impart to you some spiritual gift to make you strong—that is, that you and I may be mutually encouraged by each other's faith.' Getting together with other Christians and sharing experiences, prayer, fears, sorrows, joys, being open with a group of other people, is a mutually encouraging experience. It is not a one way traffic. Paul almost fell into the trap of thinking that it was, but he corrects his own 'so that I may impart' to read, 'that is, that you and I may be mutually...' In such a fellowship nobody loses—everybody gains.

We have mentioned Hebrews 10:24-25 before but it finds a place here in a selection of biblical motives for encouragement:

> Let us consider how we may spur one another on towards love and good deeds. Let us not give up meeting together, as some are in the habit of doing, but let us encourage one another—and all the more as you see the Day approaching.

You can't encourage effectively without being together, though letters are a valuable alternative. The opposite of 'failing to meet' in this extract is not 'meeting' but 'encouraging'. So once again the very fact of sharing fellowship has this upbuilding effect. A solemn note is then sounded as we are reminded that the Day, the end of all things, is slowly approaching. We are nearer than they were. Let us then all the more encourage one another.

## Shelley's garage

Gordon had one of his rare complete Saturdays at home. The weather was fine so he was going to tidy the garden and cut the lawn in the morning and then do some long overdue simple maintenance jobs on the car in the afternoon. It was of course a great day for Shelley as she knew that Daddy couldn't really do without her and she was his number one helper. She enjoyed her ballet class on Saturday mornings but this time she was particularly glad to get home again to begin helping. She was quickly on the job, moving grass cuttings more or less tidily and even tackling a few weeds before she got bored with them.

After lunch it was the Great Treat: car-washing time. It being a warm afternoon and Shelley being resplendent in her yellow wellington boots she was allowed to help with the hosing. Obviously she got wet. Gordon knew that she meant to get wet. Shelley knew that Gordon knew that she meant to get wet and they both enjoyed keeping the secret.

When she had been dried Shelley came out once more to help yet again. But the afternoon was waning and helping gets less interesting when the exciting bits are over. So she called in at the kitchen where Margaret was making crumble. She was just in time to be allowed to spoon in two tablespoonfuls of sugar, but there didn't seem to be much more she could do.

So she went outside again. The car was standing alone on the driveway with the bonnet up and the engine open for inspection. Gordon had been about to add oil when he had been called across to talk to his next-door neighbour. Shelley stood on tiptoe and peered into the engine. It was very interesting. There was a large box with wires, a lot of wires. Upside down cups, just like the kitchen. And a long snake, curled round. And a propeller. That must be what makes the car go along. And a big plastic bottle with water in it. It *was* like the kitchen.

She wondered whether she could do anything to help. She was bored. Daddy was talking to Mr Phillips and Mummy was busy baking. Then she noticed the open lid. She *would* help. She slipped into the kitchen and took a tablespoon from the drawer and looked round the garden for some sugar. There was no sugar, but she did have a sandpit. It would do very well as pretend sugar. She spooned up some sand and carried it carefully to the car. Nobody was looking. She leaned over and, with her tongue between her lips, poured a tablespoon of sand into the oil. She went back to the sandpit and repeated the process. Two would be enough. She leaned across and stirred the sand and oil mixture with her finger. There wasn't much oil there, but the sand went black quite quickly. Like treacle.

Now Shelley was six. She was well aware of the danger she was running into. She had a strong feeling that she was doing something very wrong. A three-year-old, in her position, might have been innocent. But she was so fascinated by what she was doing that she continued to do it, smearing and stirring...

When she heard Gordon's footsteps she scuttled guiltily away, but was in time to hear Gordon's cry of anger and astonishment...

It is not our purpose to report the details of the painful interview between Gordon Barber and his daughter that afternoon, nor the extent of the invoice from the local garage when the sand had been completely removed, nor the ghastly damage that the sand would have inflicted on the bearings if the engine had been started.

The details don't matter. But the point does. Encouragement is like oil. It cools, lubricates and frees moving parts for action. Threats and every kind of discouragement are like sand in the works. We are scraped and scratched and finally grind to a halt.

Encouragement is vital because the Bible is full of it. Our Lord set us the example, so did Paul, so especially did Barnabas and many of the biblical writers. It is also vital because it works in experience. The two go together.

Those who are obliged to live without encouragement, and there are sadly far too many, grind through life in a joyless round of duty, and achieve far less than their potential.

---

Is your life lubricated or are you trying to run on a mixture of sand and gravel?
Do you know anyone who could do with some oil just now? Go and share it.

---

# 18

# 'Don't spoil them'

**A** hundred years ago, or even fifty, all this talk of encouragement would have been frowned upon, even regarded as dangerous. In Britain at least children were expected to achieve high standards. If they did, then that was merely their duty fulfilled. If they failed then they should be punished. For failure. Failure itself was not considered punishment enough.

Children brought up in this way grew to expect not praise nor encouragement, only higher and higher expectations. Failure to achieve these ever-soaring goals was almost guaranteed and the discouragement of receiving no praise accelerated the failure. But these children became parents in their turn. And, not knowing anything different, they subjected their children to the same regime. The reason for this notion was of course that children should not be spoilt, should not become proud.

It started at birth. You had to show the infant who was master. He was to be fed at precise intervals measured by your clock, not his tummy. If he cried for his food, let him cry. It would teach him patience. So perhaps an hour before each feed was due the baby became more and more frantic and the mother torn more and more in two between pity for her suffering infant and determination not to spoil him.

And, of course, you must never 'fuss'. By that the experts of the day meant physical touch, embraces, kisses, cuddles, all the things in fact that a baby needs for its growing security. Sit it on the floor and admire it at a distance, but don't spoil it.

If you praised an older child, so the theory went, he would 'get above himself'. He would become conceited and insufferable. It would be better to keep him under. Let him know his place. Similarly, children were goaded to greater and greater efforts, especially at school, by being told how wretched were their efforts, how poorly they were doing. I well remember my French teacher 'encouraging' us to do well in our exams by telling us that we were 'not fit to lick the boots of last year's 5R'. No doubt the next year's 5R were similarly unfit to perform that service to *our* boots, and so on.

Too much praise of the wrong kind of course does result in complacency. The balance between praise where it is due and firm criticism in its right place is hard to achieve, as every school-teacher and parent knows. The worst combination, but perhaps one which frequently occurred, was a perfectionist and discouraging father, anxious to 'lick the lad into shape', and a doting and flattering mother who could see no wrong in her son. A memory, yet further back than the French teacher, is of a boy of my own age (then about eight) who used to bully the younger ones, smash windows and generally behave like a character from a comic magazine. His mother would be called to the school to explain her son's behaviour and I can still hear her declaiming, 'My Peter would *never* do a thing like that'. That was a kind of 'encouragement' which her Peter would have been better without.

Garrison Keillor is an American writer and broadcaster. A year or two ago he ran a radio series in the States which was so successful that it was said that Americans were deserting their TV sets to listen to him. His stories of his hometown, Lake Wobegon, have become a legend.

Towards the end of his classic *Lake Wobegon Days*, Keillor describes how in 1980 a former Wobegonian returned to the town with ninety-five theses, intending, like Luther before him, to nail them to the church door. This he never did, but the theses were slipped under the door of Harold Starr, the editor of *Herald-Star*, with a note which dared him to publish them. He never did that either, but Keillor gives us the benefit of reading the heart-cry of a child 'properly' brought up—without encouragement. Thesis 34 reads:

> *For fear of what it might do to me, you never paid a compliment, and when other people did, you beat it away from me with a stick. "He certainly is looking nice and grown up." He'd look a lot nicer if he did something about his skin. "That's wonderful that he got that job". Yeah, well, we'll see how long it lasts. You trained me so well, I now perform this service for myself. I deflect every kind word directed to me, and my denials are much more extravagant than the praise. "Good speech." Oh, it was way too long, I didn't know what I was talking about, I was just blathering on and on, I was glad when it was over. I do this under the impression that it is humility, a becoming quality in a person. Actually, I am starved for a good word, but after the long drought of my youth, no word is quite good enough. "Good" isn't enough. Under this thin veneer of modesty lies a monster of greed...* *

* Garrison Keillor: *Lake Wobegon Days* (Faber and Faber, 1985), p.263.

A 'monster of greed' or of pride was exactly what the parents had been trying to prevent their son becoming. Extravagant praise and flattery would no doubt have produced that monster. Lack of encouragement and affirmation had had the same effect.

# Carol Jenkins on the rack

Fred and Joan Jenkins were as near average as possible without being caricatures. They had left school with one 'O' level between them, and had enjoyed a limited success in their work and leisure activities. They were both church attenders rather than enthusiastic Christians. They were not apparently ambitious people, they would never influence world affairs, but they had one passion in common: Carol.

Carol Jenkins was the focus of her parents' unexpressed, mainly unguessed ambitions. They both longed for Carol to succeed. And so far Carol had been successful. She was seventeen, nearly eighteen, tall, vivacious and not without intelligence. She had never quite grasped Gordon Barber's explanation of Truth but she did have a useful cluster of 'O' levels and was now on course for 'A' levels, a peak that neither Fred nor Joan had scaled. So they were determined that nothing should stand in the way of Carol's academic achievements. Both parents were alarmed at their daughter's religious habits, her attendance at church on Sundays when she could have been revising, and her habit of frequenting large holiday gatherings where the emphasis seemed to be very heavily on loud music and the supernatural. God and church were all very well in their place, argued Fred, but it doesn't do to get too much involved. God never intended it.

This gem of illogicality had come down in Fred's family via his grandmother and he had clung to it as a valuable defence against too much commerce with the Almighty. Needless to say, it cut very little ice with Carol.

So as the spring progressed, Fred and Joan intensified their efforts to encourage Carol to work harder and to maintain a proper attitude to her studies and her future. The two scenes that follow were typical and frequently repeated.

'Mum?'

'Yes, dear?'

'I shall never get through all this geography. I've got seven books to read—*seven*—and I haven't started one of them. It's all new stuff and he's not going to teach it. He says we'll have to pick it up ourselves.'

'You'll be all right, dear. You know you will. You got an 'A' at 'O' level, didn't you? You'll do it easily.'

'But Mum, this isn't 'O' level. It's '*A*' level. And it's the whole of Asia I've got to do, not just the Isle of Wight like you did.'

'That's a bit unkind.'

'Well, I'm sorry, but there's such a lot of it! And that's only the geography. There are two more subjects as well. And I've only got six weeks left. It's awful. It's too much. I'm going to fail all of them...'

Joan came over and put her arm round Carol's shoulder.

'You're bound to feel a bit depressed sometimes, but you'll pull through. I know you will. You'll do brilliantly. You'll be a credit to us all. All you need to do is to believe in yourself and go for it and you'll get that university place and, and...I don't know what else. You've got to believe in yourself!'

'Believe in God, you mean, Mum.'

'Well yes, of course, we all believe in God, dear.'

'I mean, to give me the strength and the inspiration to go on.'

'Yes, I think that's right. But God helps those who help themselves, you know. It says that in the Bible somewhere. And you've got it in you to get to the top. So go for the top. We shall all be proud of you. Three 'A's remember!'

'Mum, you know I can't possibly do that! I'm hopeless!'

'Well, if you don't aim high you'll never get anywhere.'

# Three weeks later

'Dad?'

'Yes?'

'I think I'm getting the idea at last.'

'Idea of what?'

'This quantum stuff.'

'No use talking to me about quantum stuff.'

'Well, I've just begun to grasp it. Three weeks to go before the exams, too. I think it's an answer to prayer. I've got through six of those seven geography books as well. Mum's right. I'm beginning to look forward to these exams. I think I could do well.'

'Now Carol, you be careful. Pride goes before a cropper. It says that in the Bible somewhere. If you go into those exams all cocky and know-it-all, you'll come down with a bump, you know.'

'But *Dad*! I'm not being cocky. I'm trying to express some confidence.'

'Confidence, is it? Well, it sounds like over-confidence to me. If you expect to do well, you'll be disappointed when the results come because you'll do worse than you expect. Now if you aim a bit lower you can't be disappointed if you drop a bit. Then if you do really well it's all pure gain. It's an insurance against disappointment.'

'But Dad, you don't believe in me!'

'No, I didn't say that. It's just that I don't want you to build up false hopes, that's all. You'll do as well as you can, I'm sure, but you're better to aim low. That's what I did.'

'Right. You aimed low and hit it. Hard.'

'That's a bit unkind.'

'Well, I'm sorry, but if you don't aim at something worthwhile you can never reach anything. You're so discouraging!'

'No, I'm not being discouraging. I'm being realistic, Carol. It's for your own good. We obviously want you to do well.'

'For my own good! It's always for my own good. Mum tells me I'm brilliant and you tell me I'm hopeless and it's all for my own good! How am I supposed to know what's for my own good?'

'I never said you were hopeless.'

'Well, you implied it. I've prayed a lot about this recently, Dad, and I really believe the Holy Spirit is saying that he wants me to do well and get somewhere for him.'

'If you spent a bit less time praying and a bit more time

revising I'd see some sense in what you say.'

'*Dad*! You don't believe in God, do you?'

'Of course we believe in God. We go to church, don't we? I don't know why you must always expect everybody else to have your particular jazzed-up form of religion. If you believe you can get through your exams on prayer without revising properly, you've got...'

'Another think coming, my girl!'

'Another think coming, my... and don't take the words out of my mouth! You'll really have to get down to it and face reality and pull your socks up and get your nose to the grindstone and your shoulder to the wheel...Carol! Carol, where are you?'

The sound of stifled sobs from the direction of Carol's bedroom.

'Fathers, do not exasperate your children.'

It says that in the Bible somewhere.

---

How can we find the balance between over-praising someone and making them conceited, and under-affirming them and making them feel unwanted?
Make a few experiments and see how you get on. But be careful!

# 19

# Be practical

So far we have looked at what encouragement is (and what it is not), the reasons for its centrality in Christian fellowship (scriptural and practical reasons), examples of how it works in the lives of the people of Canwell Park and particularly in the life of that great encourager, Barnabas. We have ranged fairly widely and picked up a few hints on the way as to how encouragement can be handed on. The time has now come to sum up some of those ways and means and add a few more by way of example.

So, leaving aside the theory and the history, let's be practical. You want to do a bit of encouraging? Fine! Here are some suggestions.

# 1 Stir up the gift

We have already noticed that encouragement is one of the gifts of the Spirit, listed by Paul in Romans 12 (verse 8). Such a gift may be given at a particular point in your life so that you recognize it at once. It may be given for a specific purpose. It may be withdrawn again, when the purpose has been fulfilled. God's work in all this is sovereign and we need to cultivate an awareness of what is going on. We can talk to him about it, of course, discuss the matter and listen for his answers. Talk to and pray with others and get their insights too.

The gift may not be given suddenly, however. It may develop gradually. Some people seem to have a 'natural' ability to encourage others, and the Spirit of God transforms that ability into a supernatural one. In either case the gift is precious and needs to be stirred up and used frequently. In 1 Corinthians 12 Paul called upon his readers eagerly to desire the greater gifts (verse 31). He didn't say which they were. 'Those able to help others' appeared in his list earlier (verse 28). Was not encouragement a great gift?

# 2 Develop the ability

What about those who do not appear to have a specific gift of encouragement? Are they to forget the idea? By no means. The many calls to encourage throughout the Bible were not addressed to the special people but to everyone. Even if you are not gifted as a latter-day Barnabas you are not dismissed from the privilege of doing what you can as a member of the body of Christ, the fellowship of encouragers. It may be harder for you, and you won't do as well as the gifted person, but the practical suggestions which follow apply equally to the gifted and the not-so-gifted. We all do the encouraging—God does the rest according to his economy.

# 3 Develop a positive frame of mind

It is hard to help others to be positive if you are negative yourself. The pessimist makes a poor encourager. It may be contrary to your nature to take an optimistic stance. Test yourself on this scrap of dialogue:

> *'I like the dark days of winter.'*
> *'Why is that?'*
> *'Because I get to see the sunrise more often.'*

If you are a natural optimist you will probably warm to that—it chimes in with your mood. If you are a natural pessimist you will see through it at once and mark it down as a mental conjuring trick. Don't we see the sunset too? In the winter we don't often see the sun at all...

But whether you are naturally sunny or gloomy you can apply yourself to improving, and with the help of God and the benefit of your friends, you will succeed. And one way to improve your own cheerfulness is to encourage someone else. Try it and see.

One word of warning—don't overdo it. The person who is perennially jolly is a pain in the neck. We call him 'Uncle Fred' in our family. He is an unwelcome guest.

# 4 Daily

If you are the kind of person who finds Lent helpful (or even if you're not!), try giving some encouragement every day as a lenten 'fast' rather than giving something up. Better still, do it every day of the year! Who have you encouraged today?

# 5 Appreciate, don't flatter

This has been a thread which has appeared frequently and is bound up with the very meaning of encouragement—realism, truth. Avoid flattery and sickly or sentimental praise. Perhaps this too begins with your opinion of yourself; not too high (you are a sinner like the rest of us), nor too low (Christ died for you, so you matter enormously), but just right. 'Do not think of yourself more highly than you ought, but rather think of yourself with sober judgment...' (Romans 12:3). Then, even if it is painful to you, be ready to tell the truth to your friend. Who can say it better than Solomon?

> *Better is open rebuke*
> *than hidden love.*
> *The kisses of an enemy may*
> *be profuse,*
> *but faithful are the wounds*
> *of a friend.*

> (Proverbs 27:5-6)

# 6 Give reasons

There is no need to labour this point again (see chapter 16). Perhaps we should bear in mind the old verse, supposedly found in an examination paper. Did it originate in Punch?

> *'O cuckoo, should I call thee bird,*
> *Or but a wandering voice?*
> *State the alternative preferred*
> *With reasons for your choice.'*

Always be ready to give the reason for your encouragement. Avoid the empty 'Cheer up, it may never happen' approach.

# 7 The value of the well-chosen word

It is not always necessary to say a lot. In fact it's often better to say little. Whatever words you do say by way of encouragement should be well chosen and appropriate. Remember who you are talking too. Don't compliment a teenage girl on her biceps, nor an anorexic on how slim she looks.

> *A man finds joy in giving an*
> *apt reply—*
> *and how good is a timely*
> *word!*

*A word aptly spoken*
*is like apples of gold in*
*settings of silver.*

(Proverbs 15:23; 25:11)

# 8 The value of well-chosen silence

Better to say nothing than to say the wrong thing. And if you're one of those people who whenever they open their mouth, put their foot in it, make a conscious effort to say less. Ask people about themselves and be ready to listen to their answers. Even if you've heard it all before and you can guess what's coming next, pay your friend the compliment of listening with attention.

When the words are not flowing on either side, don't worry. Even when your golden apples desert you, your *presence* is encouraging. This is especially true in times of sorrow. There may not be much that you can say, apart from platitudes that are better left unsaid, but just *being there* is all that is needed.

# 9 Don't squash people

Matthew takes the words of Isaiah and applies them to Jesus:

*He will not quarrel or cry out;*
*no-one will hear his voice in*
*the streets.*
*A bruised reed he will not*
*break,*
*and a smouldering wick he*
*will not snuff out.*

(Matthew 12:19-20)

Jesus was concerned to tend and care for people, not to put them down. He knew just how easy it is to extinguish the smouldering embers of someone's faith, or even self respect.

Listen to children trying to establish themselves in each other's estimation. Almost every new snippet of information, eagerly offered, is greeted with a sneering, 'I know'. It is extremely annoying to be told that your friend knows everything you tell him, especially when you strongly suspect that he doesn't! The temptation is then to score points in return, which leads to the very opposite of encouragement.

So when your friend gives you a glowing and excited description of his flight over New York at 39,000 feet and how the whole city was laid out below him like a map, please avoid deflating him with, 'Oh yes, we often do that trip. It *is* impressive the first time, isn't it?' And if someone tells you a bit of recent news that you have just already heard, why not try to appreciate being told it, instead of saying, 'Yes, I *know*', which really means, 'I knew already. You can't tell *me* anything.'

Build up. Support. Fan into flame. Lift. Stand back and let them grow.

# 10 Believe in people

The positive side of not breaking the bruised reed is to believe in people. Give them responsibility. Allow them to make their own mistakes. Don't keep checking up on them. Yes, of course you can do the job better yourself, but we are not here on earth merely to do jobs more and more efficiently. Perhaps some efficiency will need to be sacrificed in favour of encouragement.

Finally, three examples of specifics:

# 11 Call names

Not rude names of course, but using someone's name when you are talking to them is reassuring and encouraging. Not just, 'Hello' but 'Hello, Jane'. Very simple. Many people do it naturally. Americans are especially good at it, the British rather less so.

Again a word of warning is in order. If you overdo it, using someone's name can become a means of putting them down. It depends a lot on the tone of voice and the content of the communication, but to add someone's name to the end of each sentence makes it sound as if you are claiming some kind of superiority. 'Hello, Jane. I'm glad to see you. How are you, Jane? It's a long time since we've met. You're looking well, Jane.' See what I mean?

But to avoid using the name altogether is to lose an important means of establishing a relationship.

# 12 Meet people

Another simple action, yet easily neglected. When Paul and his companions emerged from the sea after their shipwreck in Malta, they were still a great distance from Rome. He survived rain, snakebite and all the perils of a long journey (including another sea voyage), and so went to Rome.

> *The brothers there had heard that we were coming, and they travelled as far as the Forum of Appius and the Three Taverns to meet us. At the sight of these men Paul thanked God and was encouraged.*

(Acts 28:15)

A familiar idea, but so important. 'Go and meet them'. What an affirmation, when people come out of their way to meet us, at the station, at the bus stop, or even the corner of the road.

# 13 Send cards

Yes, birthday cards and anniversary cards and postcards when you're on holiday. This can be a small but important ministry. It means that you have to be well organized, keep lists or card indexes or data on your computer. It's important to be regular and not to miss, because people come to expect you to remember. Christmas and Easter are less important perhaps because there's a welter of cards flying about, but Mother's and Father's days are good to remember as well as wedding anniversaries. And why not keep a stock of small illustrated cards to express thanks, sympathy, prayer support or just 'hello' occasionally? It all helps.

These are just a few ideas. There are plenty more, but perhaps these will help you to develop your own style of encouraging.

It may be that you are rather disturbed at there being thirteen suggestions listed. So here is another:

# 14 Stop being superstitious

Which ideas in this chapter are new to you?
Which appeal to you?
Make a short list of your own preferred practical means of encouraging.

# 20
# A slice of real life

The time is 11.15. The family service has just finished and the church is alive with small groups of people, drinking coffee and relaxing together before going home for Sunday lunch.

It is St Barnabas' day and Timothy has been preaching about Barnabas and encouragement. Cyril Kent and his wife Edith are talking to Diana Monteith.

'That was a lovely sermon your husband preached this morning dear. It must be wonderful to live with Timothy—he's very like Barnabas himself isn't he?'

'Not always! He's sometimes in need of a bit of affirmation himself, you know. You've no idea how insecure he is when he's just finished preaching. He's worried about what people will think of what he's said. I'm not going to make a comparison, Edith, but if anyone is fortunate in having a good husband, I should have thought it was you. I think Cyril is marvellous and I don't mind saying it to his face!'

Cyril is obviously confused by this sudden turn of events and goes an odd shade of pink.

'You musn't say that sort of thing, Diana. I shall get ideas above my station. Besides, it isn't true. I'm only one of the Lord's lowly servants.'

'Exactly, and that is the highest praise you could give yourself. You're so humble that you don't appreciate how good you are.'

'I'm sure you mean well, but I must seriously ask you not to talk like that. Satan is always on the look-out for people like me and I know how easy it is to be tempted to pride. If you ask me, there's too much emphasis on encouragement in this church at the moment. It's becoming a fad. People can't think about anything else. You can't talk to anyone without being encouraged about something. It's like being hunted. When I see someone coming I dive for cover in case they're going to encourage me!'

'Oh *Cyril*!' Edith is rocking with half-amused, half-embarrassed laughter, but Cyril is warming to his subject.

'It reminds me of the old joke, you know: "She's a wonderful woman. She lives for others. You can recognize the others by the hunted look on their faces." But seriously, I do think we're overdoing it. It will become a matter of "I'll scratch your back if you'll scratch mine".'

'You told me what you think just now, so I'll tell you what I think.' Diana believes that she knows Cyril well enough to speak plainly. 'I think you're an old Scrooge. Marvellous as a husband, and an old Scrooge when it comes to admitting it. I think you ought to face the fact that you are marvellous and admit it. You don't need to take the credit. It's all God's doing anyway. "All things come from you and of your own have we given you." So enjoy who you are in Christ and let us enjoy you as well.'

147

For once, Cyril is silenced.

# 'It's always the Bible'

The sound of animated conversation and laughter from groups of excited people is not music to the ears of Gina Holwell. Timothy has asked them to look back over the year and review the encouragement they have received. There's not much encouragement in having a barrier between herself and Jane. It's as high as ever. She's been some use to Margaret Barber, she supposes, but *she* seems to have got stuck again now. And no amount of Barnabas-talk and encouragement will bring Andrew back... Gina walks suddenly and quickly home.

Meanwhile Gordon Barber is doing his best to develop the theme of the sermon with Fred and Joan Jenkins.

'It's all very well,' Fred is complaining, 'all this talk about encouragement. But it's in the Bible, isn't it? I only come to church on highdays and holidays and when I do, it's always the Bible.'

'*Fred*!' Joan, in her disparaging role.

'Well, it is. Nothing to do with real life. It's all about Barnabas, who was a saint, and we don't grow saints on trees round here.'

'*Fred*!'

'What kind of encouragement is there for people like us? All the church does is to take collections to buy a new organ and give teenage girls giddy ideas about being filled with the Spirit. Fill her with some common sense, that's what she needs.'

'*Fred*!'

'And stop saying, "Fred" like that! Look, Mr Barber, what encouragement is there for me? Eh? I mean, I need some. Go on, encourage me.'

'Well, Carol has done well with her 'A' levels.'

'She says it's no thanks to me. Says I tried to discourage her.'

'I think you should be grateful for a lovely wife and daughter.' Joan smiles sheepishly.

'You don't have to live with them.'

'To be quite honest, I think whatever I say, you will have

an answer for it.'

'Well, I'm glad somebody's honest. Come on Joan, let's get back to the baked beans.'

'*Fred*! You know it's roast beef.'

'Mr Barber, if you can give me ten things to be encouraged about next month, I'll join this church.'

'Please call me Gordon. You're on!'

# Never mind the quality...

Bob Renshaw is having little or no success with Mrs Beesley.

'The New Testament is full of encouragement. The Vicar was just giving the example of Barnabas, the son of encouragement.'

'Oh, he wanders on and on, does the Vicar. Canon George was lovely. You could set your clocks by his sermons. Always finished at five to eleven, on the dot. Now *that's* what I call encouraging. You knew where you were with him. He was a good man was Canon George.'

'Isn't Mr Monteith a good man?'

'Oh yes, I dare say he is, but you never know what he's going to do next!'

'Didn't Canon George ever preach about Barnabas on St Barnabas' day?'

'Oh yes, he did. Every year. Lovely it was. Always the same sermon. About encouragement. Always finished at five to eleven.'

'But Mr Monteith has preached about encouragement today.'

'He went on till nearly ten past, didn't he?'

Bob remembers that he needs to be somewhere else.

# Newly remodelled wife

Mrs Staindrop is surrounded as usual by a crowd of young people—Gavin, of course, Carol Jenkins, Rachel, Sharon and several more. It has to be admitted that they are laughing at her as well as with her. Her quaint old-fashioned expressions and her fund of humour keep them in almost continuous mirth.

She wipes her eyes from too much laughing.

'One thing I meant to say to you, Carol,' regaining her breath with difficulty, 'is how glad I am that you did so well in your exams. You're a credit to us all. And Gavin, you did even better. You'll be back here directly in your caps and gowns, I shouldn't wonder.'

Carol and Gavin quite spontaneously descend on the smiling old lady from opposite sides and hug her and deliver a kiss on either side of her face.

'Mrs Staindrop, you're a gem! We couldn't do without you!'

The said Mrs Staindrop laughs so loudly with pleasure at this that all eyes are turned to the extraordinary sight.

Timothy, with Vivien and Walter James, positively beams with pleasure.

'Who would possibly have thought twelve months ago that that lonely, shrivelled up old thing in a wheelchair would become the life and soul of the party with a gang of youth fellowship people hanging on every word she says? It's amazing! It's a work of the Holy Spirit.'

'Yes, it is, Tim, but you had something to do with it too. It was you, wasn't it, who put Gavin Morrison in touch with the Staindrops? I think that was a *very* wise move.'

'Thank you, Walter. It seems to have worked, anyway. And while we're on the subject of saying encouraging things...Vivien, you seem to be a new person these days...'

'It's the hair-do.' Walter ducks to avoid the handbag aimed at his head.

'The hair-do is a symptom, not the cause. But it's true, I really do feel as if I'm starting a new life. It's a long story and I think it's only just beginning. But it's Jane Goodrich I have to thank.'

'Jane?'

'Yes, you see...*Jane!* Come and hear some home truths!'

Jane approaches with a quizzical expression and a cup of coffee.

'Miss Goodrich.' Walter adopts a mock-serious tone. 'I have just introduced to our vicar my newly remodelled wife. We wish to acknowledge before witnesses that the refit was largely due to your influence.'

Vivien beams broadly and puts an affectionate arm round Jane's shoulders.

'Oh, don't be ridiculous! All I did was to be so tactless that I made you lose your temper with me.'

'Just what was needed!'

'But I can't take any credit for that!'

'You've been trying to help me for ages and I was too stubborn to realize it.'

'That's because I was too clumsy in my way of doing it.'

'And you've been praying for me for years, haven't you?'

'Well, that's no more than anyone else would do.'

Walter raises his eyes imploringly to the roof.

'There's no chink in her armour. Every compliment, every word of thanks, bounces off and comes back at you. It's like playing Ivan Lendl on the Centre Court ...'

Another group breaks into delighted laughter.

# 'I think he has already'

Jane, Walter and Vivien have gone home. Gordon and Margaret are counting the collection. Timothy sits down in a chair at the back of the church and feels suddenly empty. Encouragement? A few people laughing together perhaps. Is that all? Is that all it amounts to really, all this positive effort and prayerful affirmation? Gina and Jane are still not talking to one another. Mrs Beesley will never stop talking about Canon George.

But I haven't heard much about St Peter's recently. That's encouraging anyway. At least it's a slice of real life here.

'It's nice here now.'

He looks up. Shelley Barber is standing beside him, regarding him seriously.

'Hello, it's my best friend Shelley. Yes, it is nice here. But why did you say "now"?'

'Because it wasn't used to be. People weren't very friendly. And Daddy was always too busy to talk to me. But it's nice now.'

'Do you know why?'

Shelley purses her lips and nods vigorously.

'Why then?'

'It's him, isn't it?'

'Who?'

'Barnabas.'

'Really?'

'Yes. It's his church, isn't it?'

'Well, it is called St Barnabas, yes. But it's God's church.'

'Does God live here?'

'Yes, he lives everywhere, especially where Christians love him and love each other.'

'Then he lives here. Aren't you glad?'

'Yes, I'm very glad.'

'Even when people are silly?'

'Yes, even when people are silly, because what matters is that God loves us even when we're silly.'

'And naughty?' This a little anxiously.

'Yes, he forgives us when we're sorry.'

'I was naughty with Daddy's car.'

'I heard about that.'

'But I was sorry and God forgave me and so did Daddy.' A pause. 'Where is Barnabas?'

'He's in heaven. But there's a picture of him in that window over there.'

'Can I wave to him?'

'I don't see why not. But he won't wave back.'

'I think he has already.'

Look back over the past six months.
Can you remember what/who has encouraged you?
How many people have you encouraged? Go on, admit it and be thankful!

# Barnabas:
# the facts

## Where to find the doings of Barnabas

| | |
|---|---|
| Acts 4:36-37 | Introduced. He sells a field and gives the proceeds to the church. |
| Acts 9:27 | He introduces Saul (Paul) to the Jerusalem church. |
| Acts 11:22-24 | He encourages the church at Antioch. |
| Acts 11:25-26 | He brings Saul to Antioch. |
| Acts 11:29-30 | Antioch Christian aid sent to Jerusalem with Barnabas and Saul. |
| Acts 12:25 | They return to Antioch, bringing John Mark with them. |

| | |
|---|---|
| Acts 13:1-3 | Barnabas and Saul are called by the Spirit to take the gospel abroad. |
| Acts 13:4-12 | Cyprus. Elymas the sorcerer blinded. |
| 13-52 | At Antioch in Pisidia. Paul's sermon. They speak boldly and encourage the believers (v. 43) but they are expelled (vv. 50-51). |
| Acts 14:1-7 | At Iconium they preach boldly again, but a plot to stone them drives them away. |
| 8-20 | At Lystra. A man healed. Barnabas called Zeus (v. 12). Paul is stoned— they leave for Derbe. |
| 21-28 | They return the way they had come, appointing elders in the churches and return to Antioch. |

Acts 15:1-35    THE COUNCIL OF JERUSALEM

| | |
|---|---|
| 1-4 | Dispute about circumcision. Paul and Barnabas are sent to Jerusalem to support the Gentile cause. |
| 12 | Paul and Barnabas report the works of God. |
| 22 | The Council's letter sent to Antioch with Paul and Barnabas. |
| 25-26 | Referred to as 'dear friends who have risked their lives'. |
| 35 | They remain in Antioch, teaching and preaching. |

| | |
|---|---|
| Acts 15:36-41 | Barnabas and Paul quarrel over John Mark. Barnabas goes with John Mark to Cyprus. |
| 1 Corinthians 9:6 | Paul and Barnabas work for their living (discussion of apostleship). |
| Galatians 2:1-21 | Paul visits Jerusalem with Barnabas |

and they are well received, but Barnabas is deceived by the hypocrisy of Peter (v. 11).

Colossians 4:10    Mark shown to be cousin to Barnabas.

2 Timothy 4:11    Paul is reconciled to John Mark and describes him as helpful.

# Words of

The Bible must surely be the most encouraging book in the world. It teems with words and ideas which convey encouragement, strength, comfort, cheer, and so on. Some words are used only once or twice. Others are used very many times. An exhaustive list would be vast and very complicated, but to give a taste of how

| Hebrew and meaning | Example | A V / K J V |
|---|---|---|
| *balag* brighten up | Job 9:27 | comfort |
| *chazaq* strengthen, harden | 1 Samuel 30:6 | encouraged |
| *nacham* comfort sigh | Psalm 119:76 | comfort |
| *nechamah* consolation | Job 6:10 | comfort |
| *saad* support refresh | Song of Solomon | comfort |

## Greek and meaning

| | | |
|---|---|---|
| *eupsycheo* be refreshed, braced up | Philippians 2:19 | be of good comfort |
| *tharseō* be courageous, hearty | Mark 10:49 | be of good comfort |
| *paraineō* exhort, recommend, admonish | Act 27:22 | exhort |
| *parakaleō* call near, exhort, urge | Acts 16:40 | comforted |
| *paraklēsis* entreaty, calling near | Acts 13:15 | exhortation |

# encouragement

the Lord himself views the subject of encouragement in both Testaments, here is a selection of words. One reference to each is given as a sample. A concordance will provide many more. Four parallel translations are given here, again to provide a feel for the words used:

| RSV | NIV | TEV/GNB |
| --- | --- | --- |
| be of good cheer | change my expression and smile | smile |
| strengthened | found strength | God gave him courage |
| comfort | comfort | comfort |
| consolation | consolation | leap for joy |
| refresh | refresh | refresh |

| RSV | NIV | TEV/GNB |
| --- | --- | --- |
| be cheered | be cheered | be encouraged |
| take heart | cheer up! | cheer up! |
| bid | urge | beg |
| exhorted | encouraged | spoke word of encouragement |
| exhortation | encouragement | encouragement |

| Greek and meaning | Example | AV/KJV |
|---|---|---|
| *paraklētos* one called along-side, advocate. Used here of the Holy Spirit. | John 14:16, 26; 15:26; 16:7 | Comforter |
| *paramythion* solace | Philippians 2:1 | consolation |
| *paregoria* soothing | Colossians 4:11 | comfort |
| *protrepō* exhort | Acts 18:27 | wrote, exhorting |

The Hebrew words *nacham* and *nechamah* are clearly related, as are the Greek words *parakaleō*, *paraklēsis* and *paraklētos*. They are obviously of the same family and are included here because they seem to be at the centre of the meaning of encouragement and because Barnabas is called 'Son of *paraklēsis*' in Acts 4:36. J. B. Phillips translates *paraklētos* with the beautiful phrase, 'the One Who is coming to stand by you'.

| RSV | NIV | TEV/GNB |
|---|---|---|
| Counsellor | Counsellor | Helper |
| comfort | comfort | great help |
| encouragement | encouragement | makes you strong |
| encouraged | encouraged | helped him by writing |

A general survey of all the words used above suggests that encouragement is:

1 Necessary and much in demand.
2 Derived from God himself, the Encourager.
3 Something that will benefit the encouraged, not merely with good feelings but with renewed vigour.
4 Something which has real *content*, sometimes almost abrasive but certainly with backbone.
5 Something which results in joy and refreshment.
It is not an optional extra, but a central feature of truly biblical relationships.